S.Y. VIDAL

LIFE'S A MESS AND THEN YOU TURN 40

rosemary woodlands
publishing

IF YOU CAN BE ANYTHING, BE INCLUSIVE
SI PUEDES SER CUALQUIER COSA, SÉ INCLUSIVO

Published by Rosemary Woodlands Publishing
San Juan, Puerto Rico USA
www.rosemarywoodlands.com
First Edition
ISBN: 979-8-9911231-2-9
Printed in the United States of America

This book is a work of non-fiction. Names, characters, places, and incidents are the product of the author's experience. Any resemblance to actual persons, living or dead, or actual events is intentional.

For those who woke up at 40 and found themselves in the middle of life's twisted joke.

"At 40, life reveals itself as a dark comedy, full of unexpected plot twists and ironic laughs. It's messy, unpredictable, and often absurd, but it's your story, and it's worth every moment."

- S.Y. Vidal

CONTENTS

LESSON 1 - *PG 17*

EMBRACING IMPERFECTIONS

LESSON 2 - *PG 21*

FINDING STRENGTH IN VULNERABILITY

LESSON 3 - *PG 24*

THE POWER OF FORGIVENESS

LESSON 4 - *PG 28*

BUILDING HEALTHY BOUNDARIES

LESSON 5 - *PG 32*

UNDERSTANDING TOXICITY & HOW TO OVERCOME IT

LESSON 6 - *PG 36*

THE IMPORTANCE OF SELF-LOVE

LESSON 7 - *PG 39*

LESSONS FROM SIBLINGS & FRIENDS

LESSON 8 - *PG 42*

NAVIGATING FAMILY DYNAMICS

LESSON 9 - *PG 46*

LEARNING TO COMMUNICATE EFFECTIVELY

LESSON 10 - *PG 50*

ACCEPTING CHANGE & MOVING FORWARD

LESSON 11 - *PG 53*

NAVIGATING EDUCATION AS A QUEER STUDENT

LESSON 12 - *PG 56*

THE VALUE OF EDUCATION (FORMAL & INFORMAL)

LESSON 13 - *PG 60*

CULTIVATING RESILIENCE

LESSON 14 - *PG 63*

DEALING WITH PEER PRESSURE

LESSON 15 - *PG 66*

THE ROLE OF MENTORS

LESSON 16 - *PG 69*

UNDERSTANDING & EMBRACING DIVERSITY

LESSON 17 - *PG 73*

MANAGING FINANCES EARLY ON

LESSON 18 - *PG 77*

THE IMPORTANCE OF DREAMING BIG

LESSON 19 - *PG 81*

BALANCING AMBITION WITH SELF-CARE

LESSON 20 - *PG 85*

BUILDING LIFELONG FRIENDSHIPS

LESSON 21 - *PG 88*

FINDING YOUR PASSION

LESSON 22 - *PG 91*

THE IMPORTANCE OF NETWORKING

LESSON 23 - *PG 95*

LEARNING FROM FAILURES

LESSON 24 - *PG 98*

DEVELOPING LEADERSHIP SKILLS

LESSON 25 - *PG 102*

WORK-LIFE BALANCE

LESSON 26 - *PG 106*

THE POWER OF PERSISTENCE

LESSON 27 - *PG 109*

ADAPTING TO TECHNOLOGICAL CHANGES

LESSON 28 - *PG 113*

THE VALUE OF CONTINUOUS LEARNING

LESSON 29 - PG 117

SETTING & ACHIEVING GOALS

LESSON 30 - PG 121

THE ROLE OF GRATITUDE IN SUCCESS

LESSON 31 - PG 125

THE IMPORTANCE OF EMPATHY

LESSON 32 - PG 129

KEEPING ROMANCE SPICY & ALIVE IN YOUR RELATIONSHIP

LESSON 33 - PG 134

THE ART OF SAYING NO

LESSON 34 - PG 137

MANAGING LIFE'S TRANSITIONS

LESSON 35 - PG 140

THE ROLE OF COMMUNITY & GIVING BACK

LESSON 36 - *PG 144*

PRACTICING MINDFULNESS & MEDITATION

LESSON 37 - *PG 148*

HEALTH & WELLNESS

LESSON 38 - *PG 151*

THE JOY OF TRAVEL & EXPLORATION

LESSON 39 - *PG 155*

FINDING PEACE IN SOLITUDE

LESSON 40 - *PG 159*

LIVING AUTHENTICALLY

INTRODUCTION

So, here we are. Me, staring down the barrel of 40, and you, along for the ride, ready to soak up the wisdom I've managed to scrape together over the years. I know, I know—another "life lessons" book. But hang tight. This isn't your typical self-help snooze fest filled with clichés and motivational poster quotes. No, this is real talk from someone who's waded through the muck, wrestled with their demons, and come out the other side with a few scars and a hell of a lot of stories.

Let's get one thing straight: life is messy. It's less like a well-curated Instagram feed and more like the blooper reel of a reality TV show. There are moments of sheer brilliance, sure, but there are also plenty of faceplants and awkward silences. And that's okay. In fact, it's more than okay—it's essential. Because if there's one thing I've learned before hitting the big 4-0, it's that the beauty of life is in its imperfection. It's in those unscripted moments that we find our true selves, the raw, unfiltered versions that no amount of Photoshop can touch up.

When I was a kid, I thought turning 40 meant you had everything figured out. Spoiler alert: it doesn't. What it does mean is you've got a decent handle on what really matters, like knowing the perfect response to an unsolicited "Hey, you up?" text (it's a well-timed "New phone, who dis?"). You also learn the importance of setting boundaries —especially with family members who still think it's okay to comment on your life choices at every Thanksgiving dinner. Newsflash, Aunt Karen: my career in commercial real estate is not up for debate, just like your 'special' jello salad isn't up for seconds.

And speaking of family, let's dive into the first batch of lessons I've picked up from that wonderful circus. From surviving toxic parents to understanding the true meaning of self-love, these early chapters are all about navigating the wild rollercoaster that is family life. Trust me, by the end of this, you'll either feel validated in your own experiences or, at the very least, know you're not alone in wondering if you were switched at birth.

In the spirit of keeping it real, I'll be sharing some personal stories—some funny, some painful, and some downright bizarre. Like the time I realized that trying to be perfect for others was about as effective as using a chocolate teapot. Or the moment I discovered that forgiveness isn't just for saints and martyrs but for regular folks like us who want to sleep soundly at night.

My previous books, "Who Needs Santa? & Other Lessons in Surviving Toxic Parents" and "Who Needs Santa? Shadows of Shame: Overcoming Toxic Shame & Embracing Self-Worth," have tackled some of these themes in different ways. In "Who Needs Santa?", I delved into the harsh realities of growing up with parental neglect and abuse, navigating the long-term effects of living in survival mode, and the journey towards healing and self-sufficiency. "Who Needs Santa? Shadows of Shame" explored the deep-rooted impacts of toxic shaming and the path to reclaiming self-worth and building a life rooted in authenticity and self-respect.

This book takes it a step further, combining those lessons with the added perspective of hitting a milestone birthday. It's about facing the chaos head-on, finding humor in the absurd, and learning to thrive in spite of—and sometimes because of—the mess. Life doesn't come with a manual, but if it did, it would probably be filled with crossed-out sentences, coffee stains, and doodles in the margins. And that's exactly what makes it worth living.

So grab a cup of coffee, a glass of wine, or whatever gets you through the day, and settle in. Cheers to the messy, the imperfect, and the wonderfully human journey we're all on. Your next adventure starts here.

EMBRACING IMPERFECTION

erfection. The unattainable unicorn we all chase, thinking it holds the key to acceptance, love, and maybe even a gold star sticker. Growing up, I was no different. I believed that if I could just be perfect—get straight A's, excel in every extracurricular, and never, ever disappoint anyone—I'd unlock the secret to eternal approval. Spoiler alert: it doesn't work that way. And thank Gaga for that, because who wants to live life as a Stepford human?

Let's rewind to my younger years. Picture it: a lanky, eager-to-please kid with a backpack heavier than his self-esteem issues. My days were a blur of meticulously organized binders, color-coded study schedules, and a relentless pursuit of the next accolade. At home, it was about being the perfect child—obedient, respectful, and never the cause of any family drama (which, let's be real,

17

was unavoidable in my family). The goal? To be seen, appreciated, and above all, loved.

But here's the thing about chasing perfection: it's exhausting. And it's a bit like trying to nail Jell-O to a wall. The more I strived to be perfect, the more I felt like I was failing. Any minor slip-up felt like the end of the world. Got a B+ on a test? Cue the dramatic internal monologue about being a colossal failure. Didn't make the varsity team? Clearly, I was destined for a life of mediocrity.

It took me years—decades even—to realize that perfection is an illusion, a mirage in the desert of life. The turning point? Let's just say it involved third grade, Mrs. Mikesell, and a chili dog.

Picture it: a quiet afternoon in the classroom. We're all gathered around for story time, and I've got a belly full of regret (and chili dogs). Suddenly, my stomach decides to stage a rebellion, and before I know it, I let out a fart loud enough to wake the dead. The room goes silent. My face turns every shade of red known to humanity. I'm mortified, ready to dig a hole and bury myself right there next to the crayons.

But then, Mrs. Mikesell, in her infinite wisdom, does something unexpected. She laughs. Not a mean, mocking laugh, but a genuine, hearty chuckle. "Well, I guess the chili dogs are winning today!" she says, breaking the tension and turning my social death sentence into a moment of hilarity. The class bursts into laughter, and suddenly, my epic fart is the funniest thing that happened all year.

That was the first crack in my perfectionist armor. I realized that it's okay to be flawed, to have moments that aren't Instagram-perfect. In fact, it's more than okay—it's what makes us human.

Embracing imperfection has been a game-changer. It's like trading in a straightjacket for a comfy pair of sweats. When you let go of the need to be perfect, you open yourself up to a world of authenticity and confidence. You start to see that your worth isn't tied to your achievements but to who you are, warts and all.

Practical Advice

1. **Embrace Flaws and Learn from Mistakes:** We all fuck up. The key is to view mistakes as opportunities for growth rather than reflections of your inadequacy. Did you burn dinner? Great, now you know how not to cook lasagna. Did you botch a work presentation? Fantastic, that's one less way to present next time. Each mistake is a stepping stone to becoming more resilient and resourceful.

2. **Surround Yourself with Accepting People:** Ditch the toxic folks who expect perfection and instead, find your tribe—people who love you for your quirks, flaws, and all. They're the ones who'll laugh with you when things go sideways and cheer you on when you're feeling low. True friends see the beauty in your messiness and celebrate it.

3. **Set Realistic Goals and Celebrate Small Achievements:** Aim high, but keep your feet on the ground. Set achievable goals and savor the small victories along the way. Finished a daunting

project? Treat yourself. Managed to keep your houseplants alive for a month? You're a hero. Life is a series of small wins, and each one deserves recognition.

Lesson #1

Imperfection is a strength, not a weakness. It's what makes us relatable, lovable, and ultimately, human. By embracing our flaws and learning from our mistakes, we become more authentic and confident in who we are. So, here's to the beauty of imperfection and the genuine connections it fosters. Because in the grand tapestry of life, it's the imperfect threads that create the most stunning patterns.

FINDING STRENGTH IN VULNERABILITY

Vulnerability. The word alone used to make me break out in hives. To me, it screamed weakness, exposure, and a fast track to getting hurt. I spent a good chunk of my life building walls thicker than a Game of Thrones fortress to avoid being vulnerable. But here's the kicker: those walls were also keeping out the good stuff—connection, intimacy, and genuine relationships.

Let's rewind to a moment that cracked those walls wide open. It was my sophomore year of college, a time when I was convinced that appearing invincible was the key to survival. I had just bombed an important midterm, and my life felt like it was spiraling. To top it off, I was dealing with some heavy personal issues, but I wore my "everything's fine" mask like a pro. Enter my friend Jenna,

21

the kind of person who could see through my bullshit a mile away.

One night, after a few too many drinks, Jenna cornered me. "Spill it," she demanded. "I know something's up." The old me would've deflected with humor or a snarky comment, but in that moment, the dam broke. I started talking. And not just the surface-level stuff—I mean the raw, ugly, tear-streaked confessions that I'd been bottling up for months.

To my surprise, Jenna didn't flinch. She listened, really listened. And then she did something that blew my mind: she shared her own struggles. Turns out, she was dealing with a mountain of crap too. That night, over shared vulnerabilities and a lot of tissues, our friendship deepened in a way I hadn't thought possible. It was a revelation. Being vulnerable didn't make me weak—it made me human. And it forged a bond that was far stronger than any facade of invincibility ever could.

Practical Advice

1. **Share Your True Feelings with Trusted People:** It's terrifying, I know. But opening up to the right people—those who've earned your trust—can be incredibly liberating. It's like ripping off a bandage: painful at first, but ultimately healing. You'd be surprised how many people are willing to lend an ear and a shoulder when you're honest about your struggles.

2. **Understand That Everyone Has Vulnerabilities:** **Newsflash!** Nobody has their shit together all the time. Everyone has their own set of insecurities and fears. Realizing this helps you see that vulnerability isn't a solo burden but a universal experience. It's a part of being human, and it's something we all share.

3. **Use Vulnerability to Build Deeper Relationships:** True connections are built on authenticity, not bravado. When you allow yourself to be vulnerable, you invite others to do the same. This creates a space for deeper understanding and empathy. It's like emotional CPR—it brings relationships to life in the most profound way.

Lesson #2

Embracing vulnerability fosters genuine relationships and personal strength. It's not about airing your dirty laundry to the world but finding the courage to be real with those who matter. In a society obsessed with perfection, vulnerability is a rebellious act of authenticity. It strips away the masks and allows for true connection. So, here's to finding strength in our vulnerabilities and the deeper, more meaningful relationships they bring. Because at the end of the day, it's our shared humanity—not our illusions of perfection—that truly connects us.

THE POWER OF FORGIVENESS

Forgiveness. It's one of those words that gets tossed around like confetti at a New Year's party, but when it comes down to it, it's about as easy to grasp as smoke. Growing up, I thought forgiveness was for saints and doormats. I mean, why the hell should I let someone off the hook after they've screwed me over? Holding a grudge felt like the right kind of justice. But as I got older, I realized that lugging around that grudge was like carrying a backpack full of bricks—it was heavy, and the only person it was weighing down was me.

Let me take you back to high school. There was this one guy, let's call him Jake, who seemed to have it out for me. Maybe it was because I was unapologetically myself— queer, feminine, and fabulous—or maybe he was just a natural-born asshole. Either way, Jake made it his mission to make my life miserable. He'd spread rumors, throw slurs my way, and generally be a thorn in my side. I hated him with a passion that only a teenager can muster. Every time I saw his smug face, my blood boiled.

Years later, I bumped into Jake at a reunion. I was ready for the same old animosity, but something had changed. He had changed. He approached me with an awkward smile and said, "Hey, I was a real jerk back in the day. I'm sorry." I was floored. Part of me wanted to punch him in the face for all the grief he caused, but another part of me felt this weird sense of relief. His apology was like a release valve on a pressure cooker.

That night, I realized that holding onto my grudge against Jake had done nothing but keep me tethered to those shitty high school days. Forgiving him didn't mean I was condoning his behavior; it meant I was choosing to unburden myself. It was like finally dropping that backpack full of bricks.

But here's the twist: Jake wasn't just apologizing out of some newfound sense of decency. He confided in me that he had been struggling with his own identity all those years. He was gay, too, and seeing me live so openly and authentically had made him both envious and scared. His bullying was a twisted way of dealing with his own insecurities.

Forgiving Jake wasn't just about letting go of the past; it was about understanding the complexity of human behavior. It didn't excuse what he did, but it helped me see that his actions were more about his struggles than my worth. Forgiveness is for your peace, not necessarily for the other person. It's about freeing yourself from the chains of the past and allowing yourself to move forward without the weight of old resentments.

Practical Advice

1. **Forgive Yourself and Others:** We all make mistakes, and sometimes, we're our harshest critics. Start with forgiving yourself for your own screw-ups. Then, extend that grace to others. It's not about letting them off the hook; it's about letting yourself off the hook from carrying around that anger.

2. **Understand that Forgiveness Does Not Mean Forgetting:** Forgiveness is not about erasing the past or pretending it didn't happen. It's about acknowledging what happened, learning from it, and deciding not to let it control your present. You can forgive someone and still remember why they don't deserve a place in your life.

3. **Use Forgiveness as a Tool for Personal Growth:** Every time you forgive, you're practicing letting go and moving on. It's a muscle that gets stronger the more you use it. Over time, you'll find that it becomes easier to release grudges and embrace a more peaceful state of mind.

Lesson #3

Forgiveness frees you from the past and allows you to move forward. It's a gift you give yourself, a way to unshackle your heart and mind from old wounds. So, here's to forgiving those who've wronged us, not because they deserve it, but because we deserve peace. Life's too short to be weighed down by grudges. Let them go, and make space for better things ahead.

BUILDING HEALTHY BOUNDARIES

Boundaries. Not exactly the sexiest topic, but damn, are they crucial. If you've ever felt like everyone's personal assistant or found yourself drowning in commitments you never wanted to make, you know what I'm talking about. Setting boundaries is like installing a top-notch security system around your peace of mind. Without them, life can quickly turn into a chaotic mess of burnout and resentment.

Let me take you back to my early career in hospitality. Fresh out of college, I was eager to prove myself in the fast-paced world of restaurants and hotels. I was the "yes" person. Need someone to cover a double shift? Absolutely! Last-minute event planning? I'm on it! Training new staff on my day off? Of course! I was on a fast track to impressing everyone—except myself.

The problem was, my willingness to do everything and be everywhere left me with zero time for myself. My social life was non-existent, and my mental health was circling the drain. The final straw came one Friday night. I was working yet another double shift, running on fumes and caffeine. My phone buzzed with a text from a friend I hadn't seen in months: "Hey, remember what fun looks like? Wanna catch up tonight?" I stared at the screen, feeling a wave of sadness and exhaustion crash over me.

I realized then that I had no one to blame but myself. I had let my boundaries dissolve into nothingness. My inability to say no and set limits had led me straight into burnout city. So, I did something radical: I started saying no. Not all the time, but enough to reclaim my life. The first time was terrifying. My manager asked me to cover another shift, and I said, "I can't tonight. I have plans." It was the truth—I had a hot date with my couch and Netflix. But it felt like a small revolution.

Setting boundaries didn't just improve my work life; it transformed my relationships. Friends who always expected me to be available at the drop of a hat learned to respect my time. Family members who assumed I'd handle everything realized I had limits. It wasn't easy, and it didn't happen overnight, but it was worth it.

Healthy boundaries are essential for self-care and respectful relationships. They're not about shutting people out; they're about protecting your energy and ensuring that you're giving from a place of strength, not depletion.

Practical Advice

1. **Clearly Communicate Your Limits:** Be honest about what you can and cannot do. It's okay to say, "I'm sorry, but I can't commit to this right now." The people who matter will understand and respect your honesty.

2. **Respect Others' Boundaries:** Just as you need your boundaries respected, others do too. If someone says no or sets a limit, don't take it personally. It's a sign of a healthy relationship when boundaries are mutually respected.

3. **Practice Saying No Without Guilt:** No is a complete sentence. You don't owe anyone an explanation for prioritizing your well-being. Start small—decline an invitation to an event you don't want to attend or turn down an extra task at work. The more you practice, the easier it gets.

Lesson #4

Boundaries protect your well-being and foster healthy relationships. They're not about being selfish; they're about self-preservation. Setting clear limits ensures that your relationships are built on mutual respect and understanding. So, here's to drawing those lines and guarding your peace. Life's too short to be everything to everyone. Set your boundaries, and watch your world transform for the better.

UNDERSTANDING TOXICITY & HOW TO OVERCOME IT

Toxicity. It's like a slow-acting poison that seeps into your life, often without you even realizing it. Dealing with toxic individuals, especially when they're family, can feel like you're stuck in a never-ending episode of a reality TV show where everyone's fighting and no one gets voted off the island. Recognizing and overcoming toxicity is crucial for mental health, and it's a lesson I learned the hard way.

Let me take you back to a particularly rough period involving my mother. Growing up, family dynamics were a minefield, but nothing prepared me for the emotional warfare I faced when I started dating my now-husband. We had been together for a few years, and things were serious. We were about to move away for his new job, and naturally, emotions were running high. Enter my mother, in all her narcissistic glory.

It all started with a Facebook post during the 2016 presidential cycle—ah, the good old days. My mother had shared some Hillary Clinton propaganda, and my husband, being the respectful yet inquisitive man he is, questioned her about it. He wasn't disrespectful, just curious and engaged in healthy debate. But my mother saw it as a threat to her authority.

The night before we were set to move, she decided to unleash her fury. She tried to plant seeds of doubt in my mind, saying horrible things about my husband, questioning his intentions, and essentially trying to turn me against him. It was classic narcissistic behavior—manipulative, controlling, and toxic.

Something inside me snapped. I realized that if I didn't stand up to her now, she would continue to meddle in my relationships and my life. So, I did something I had never done before: I confronted her. I told her that I loved my husband and that I wasn't going to let her toxic behavior stand in the way of my happiness anymore. It was a painful conversation, and it didn't magically fix our relationship, but it was a turning point.

By setting that boundary, I took the first step in overcoming the toxicity that had been poisoning my life. I distanced myself from her manipulative behavior and focused on nurturing healthy relationships with people who respected me and my choices.

Identifying toxic behaviors and deciding to distance yourself from them isn't easy, especially when it involves family. But it's necessary. Toxicity isn't just about the person who's spewing it; it's about how you let it affect your life. By recognizing these patterns and taking action, you can protect your mental health and find a healthier, happier path forward.

Practical Advice

1. **Identify Toxic Behaviors:** Pay attention to how people make you feel. If someone consistently drains your energy, makes you feel bad about yourself, or manipulates situations to their advantage, they're toxic. Recognize these patterns and acknowledge their impact on your well-being.

2. **Distance Yourself from Toxic Individuals:** This can be challenging, especially with family. Start by setting clear boundaries and limiting your interactions with toxic individuals. If confrontation is necessary, be firm and honest about how their behavior affects you. Sometimes, reducing contact or cutting ties is the healthiest option.

3. **Seek Support from Healthy Relationships:** Surround yourself with people who uplift and support you. Lean on friends and family members who respect your boundaries and contribute positively to your life. Healthy relationships provide a solid foundation for overcoming the negative impact of toxicity.

Lesson #5

Overcoming toxicity leads to a healthier and happier life. It's about reclaiming your peace and protecting your mental health from the corrosive effects of negative influences. So, here's to recognizing the toxic patterns, standing up for yourself, and surrounding yourself with love and positivity. Life's too short to let anyone drag you down. Take control, distance yourself from the toxic, and watch your life flourish.

THE IMPORTANCE OF SELF-LOVE

Self-love. It's a term that often gets thrown around in self-help books and motivational speeches, but its significance cannot be overstated. The journey to discovering self-love, especially after years of self-criticism, is both arduous and transformative. Understanding that self-love is the bedrock upon which a happy and fulfilling life is built is crucial.

Let me recount a pivotal period in my life. For years, I was my own harshest critic. Every mistake was magnified, every flaw scrutinized. I held myself to impossibly high standards, believing that self-criticism would drive me to improve. Instead, it left me feeling perpetually inadequate and exhausted.

The turning point came during a particularly difficult time. I was struggling with a project that seemed to highlight every one of my perceived shortcomings. Frustrated and disheartened, I confided in a close friend. She listened patiently and then offered a piece of advice that changed my perspective: "You need to be kinder to yourself. Treat yourself as you would a friend."

That simple yet profound suggestion set me on a path toward self-love. I began practicing self-compassion, allowing myself the grace to make mistakes and learn from them without harsh judgment. This shift in mindset was transformative. I started to engage in activities that brought me joy and surrounded myself with positive influences that reinforced a healthier self-image.

Practical Advice

1. **Practice Self-Compassion:** Self-compassion involves treating yourself with the same kindness and understanding that you would offer to a friend. It means recognizing that everyone makes mistakes and that these mistakes do not define your worth. Instead of berating yourself for perceived failures, practice self-forgiveness and encouragement.

2. **Engage in Activities that Bring Joy:** Identify activities that genuinely bring you happiness and fulfillment. Whether it's a hobby, spending time in nature, or simply taking a break to relax, prioritize these activities in your daily life. They are essential

for recharging your mental and emotional batteries.

3. **Surround Yourself with Positivity:** The company you keep has a significant impact on your self-perception. Surround yourself with individuals who uplift and support you. Avoid those who consistently bring negativity into your life. Positive relationships foster a supportive environment where self-love can flourish.

Lesson #6

Self-love is essential for overall well-being and happiness. It is not about narcissism or self-indulgence but about recognizing your intrinsic value and treating yourself with the respect and care you deserve. By practicing self-compassion, engaging in joyful activities, and surrounding yourself with positivity, you create a strong foundation for a fulfilled and content life. Embrace self-love as a vital component of your mental and emotional health, and watch as it transforms every aspect of your existence.

LESSONS FROM SIBLINGS & FRIENDS

Siblings and friends. They're the ones who see us at our best and our worst, and they often deliver life's most profound lessons—sometimes with a swift kick in the ass. One of the most memorable lessons I learned about the importance of showing up for each other came from my little brother.

Growing up, our family wasn't exactly the picture of harmony. Our mother's moods dictated the household's atmosphere. Some years, Christmas would go uncelebrated because she "didn't feel the spirit"—usually a euphemism for some relationship drama she was embroiled in. Amidst this chaotic upbringing, my brother and I developed a thick skin and a tendency to fend for ourselves.

As adults, I thought I was doing alright in maintaining our sibling bond, given the circumstances we grew up in.

But my brother had a different perspective. One day, he called me out—hard. He was upset that I rarely called on birthdays, holidays, or just to check in. He laid it all out, and it stung. I had always assumed that, given our rough childhood, we were doing fine just keeping our heads above water.

But my brother wanted more. He wanted a relationship where we celebrated each other, showed up for each other, and created the kind of supportive family environment we never had. It was a wake-up call that made me realize how important it is to be present and involved in the lives of those we care about.

Practical Advice

1. **Cherish and Nurture These Relationships:** Siblings and friends are our chosen family. Take the time to cherish and nurture these bonds. Regular check-ins, celebrating milestones, and being there during tough times strengthen these connections.

2. **Learn from Their Experiences:** Everyone has unique life experiences and perspectives. Listen to your siblings and friends. Their stories and insights can offer valuable lessons and broaden your understanding of the world.

3. **Support Each Other Through Ups and Downs:** Life is a rollercoaster, and having a solid support system makes all the difference. Be there for each other, whether it's offering a listening ear, lending a hand, or just being present during significant moments. Your presence matters more than you realize.

Lesson #7

Siblings and friends provide lifelong lessons and unwavering support. They challenge us, teach us, and remind us of the importance of showing up for each other. My brother's confrontation was a tough pill to swallow, but it was necessary. It taught me that maintaining strong, supportive relationships requires effort and commitment. By cherishing these bonds, learning from each other, and consistently showing up, we create a network of love and support that can weather any storm. So here's to the siblings and friends who keep us grounded and remind us of the true meaning of family.

NAVIGATING FAMILY DYNAMICS

Family dynamics. They can be a wild ride, especially when your upbringing is as chaotic as a reality TV show marathon. Navigating these dynamics is key to maintaining some semblance of harmony and sanity, and it's something I had to learn through a lot of trial and error.

Growing up, my life was a whirlwind of instability. My mom had me at 17 and my dad at 19, both barely more than kids themselves. They did what they could, but more often than not, I was tossed between their new lives and new families, and primarily raised by my grandparents. My grandparents, divorced and leading separate lives, were my primary caregivers because my parents were out trying to figure out theirs.

The constant back-and-forth left me feeling like a misfit in both my parents' new families. My father remarried and started a new family, and my mother did the same. Neither household felt like home. At my father's, I faced religious persecution—anything that didn't fit into their strict beliefs was met with harsh judgment. My mother's house wasn't any better, filled with emotional and sometimes physical abuse. I was caught in a perpetual tug-of-war, never truly belonging anywhere.

One of the most memorable examples of the challenges I faced came during one of my high school musicals. Performing was one of the few things that brought me joy and a sense of accomplishment. I was excited when my father's side of the family, including my step-grandfather, decided to come see one of my shows. I thought it might be a chance to bridge some gaps and share something I loved with them.

However, the aftermath was a harsh reminder of the divide. The musical was a standard high school production, but my step-grandfather's religious convictions led him to see immorality where there was none. The day after the performance, my director gathered the cast to tell us about a complaint that had been lodged with the school. My step-grandfather had called to complain about the "sexuality and immoral topics" being displayed on stage. I was mortified. What should have been a proud moment turned into a source of shame and conflict.

On the flip side, any attempt to seek comfort at my mother's was met with emotional manipulation and disdain. She could never provide the support I needed, often too wrapped up in her own dramas to notice mine. It was a no-win situation.

Navigating these complex family dynamics taught me valuable lessons about resilience, self-worth, and not letting others define who you are. Understanding that my parents and their new families were dealing with their own issues didn't make it easier, but it provided context. I learned that it was crucial to focus on what I could control: my reactions, my goals, and my mental health.

Practical Advice

1. **Focus on Your Own Path:** Your family's drama doesn't have to be your drama. Concentrate on your own journey and what makes you happy. Use your passions and interests, like my involvement in theater, as a way to build your self-esteem and identity.

2. **Don't Internalize Their Judgments:** Just because someone in your family criticizes you or doesn't support your choices doesn't mean their opinions define you. Learn to differentiate between constructive feedback and toxic criticism. Remember, their issues are often more about them than about you.

3. **Seek Support Outside the Family:** Build a network of friends, mentors, and allies who understand and support you. These relationships can provide the encouragement and validation you might not get from your family.

4. **Set Emotional Boundaries:** While it might not be possible to confront every family member, you can set internal boundaries. Decide what behaviors you will and won't accept, and mentally distance yourself from toxic interactions.

5. **Develop Coping Mechanisms:** Find healthy ways to cope with stress and emotional pain. This could be through hobbies, exercise, meditation, or seeking professional help. Developing these mechanisms helps you maintain your mental health despite family turmoil.

Lesson #8

Healthy family dynamics lead to a supportive and loving environment, but sometimes, you have to create your own sense of family and support. My chaotic upbringing taught me that while you can't choose your family, you can choose how you respond to them. By focusing on your path, not internalizing negative judgments, seeking external support, setting emotional boundaries, and developing coping mechanisms, you can overcome tough family dynamics and build a life that reflects your values and dreams. So here's to rising above the chaos and finding your own peace and identity amidst the storm.

LEARNING TO COMMUNICATE EFFECTIVELY

Communication. It's the glue that holds relationships together, yet it's so often where things fall apart. I learned the hard way that poor communication can lead to misunderstandings, conflicts, and a whole lot of unnecessary drama. But improving my communication skills turned things around and showed me just how crucial effective communication is for healthy relationships.

Let me take you back to a particularly trying time in my early years with my now-husband. We had just moved into our first apartment together. The excitement of starting a new chapter was quickly overshadowed by the reality of merging our lives and habits. One evening, after a long day at work, I came home to find that he had rearranged the

46

entire living room. Furniture was moved, decorations were changed, and my favorite chair was nowhere to be found. I felt a wave of irritation and frustration wash over me. Without thinking, I snapped, "Why did you move everything without asking me?"

He looked taken aback and responded defensively, "I thought you'd like it. I wanted to surprise you."

That night, we barely spoke to each other, each of us nursing our own hurt feelings. The atmosphere was tense, and I realized that our communication had hit a serious snag. The next day, after some reflection, I knew we needed to talk it out. I approached him and said, "Can we talk about last night? I'm sorry for snapping. I should have asked you why you made the changes instead of assuming the worst."

He sighed, "I'm sorry too. I just wanted to make our place feel more like home. I should have checked with you first."

That conversation was a turning point. We realized that our issue wasn't about the furniture—it was about feeling considered and respected. We both needed to work on our communication skills to avoid these misunderstandings in the future.

Practical Advice

1. **Listen Actively:** Listening isn't just about hearing the words; it's about understanding the emotions and intentions behind them. When your partner or friend speaks, give them your full attention. Nod, make eye contact, and don't interrupt. Show that

you're engaged and that you care about what they're saying.

2. **Speak Clearly and Assertively:** Express your thoughts and feelings openly and honestly. Avoid passive-aggressive comments or beating around the bush. Use "I" statements to convey your perspective without blaming others. For example, say, "I feel upset when the living room is rearranged without discussing it," instead of, "You always change things without asking."

3. **Address Conflicts Directly but Respectfully:** When conflicts arise, tackle them head-on. Avoid letting resentment build up by sweeping issues under the rug. Approach the conversation with a calm demeanor and a focus on resolution. Respect the other person's viewpoint and seek a compromise that works for both parties.

Lesson #9

Effective communication fosters understanding and strengthens relationships. It's not just about talking; it's about listening, empathizing, and expressing yourself in a way that builds trust and respect. My experience with my husband taught me that good communication can turn conflicts into opportunities for growth. By listening actively, speaking clearly and assertively, and addressing conflicts directly but respectfully, you can navigate misunderstandings and build stronger, healthier relationships. Here's to mastering the art of communication and reaping the rewards of deeper connections and mutual respect.

ACCEPTING CHANGE & MOVING FORWARD

Change. It's the one constant in life that we can always count on, yet it's often the hardest to accept. Whether it's a new job, a move to a different city, or a shift in personal relationships, change can feel like stepping into the unknown. But accepting change is essential for personal development, and it's a lesson I learned through a significant life event.

A few years ago, my husband received an incredible job offer in a different city. It was an opportunity he couldn't pass up, and while I was happy for him, the thought of uprooting our lives filled me with anxiety. We had built a comfortable life where we were—friends, routines, familiarity. Moving meant leaving all that behind and starting over.

The day we packed up the last of our belongings was bittersweet. As we drove away from our old home, I couldn't shake the feeling of loss and uncertainty. But once we arrived in the new city, something amazing happened. Instead of dwelling on what we left behind, we started to embrace the possibilities ahead.

We explored our new neighborhood, met new people, and discovered hidden gems in our new city. My initial apprehension slowly gave way to excitement. I realized that this change was an opportunity to grow, both personally and as a couple. The move forced me out of my comfort zone and pushed me to adapt and thrive in a new environment.

Practical Advice

1. **Be Open to New Experiences:** When faced with change, keep an open mind. Embrace the new experiences that come your way, even if they feel uncomfortable at first. You never know what opportunities or friendships you might find.

2. **View Change as an Opportunity:** Instead of seeing change as a loss, reframe it as an opportunity for growth. Change often brings new challenges, but it also opens doors to new possibilities and experiences that you might not have considered before.

3. **Learn from Past Experiences to Navigate Future Changes:** Reflect on past changes you've navigated successfully. Use those experiences to build confidence in your ability to handle new changes. Each change you've embraced in the past has equipped you with skills and resilience that will help you in the future.

Lesson #10

Accepting change leads to growth and new opportunities. Embracing change isn't always easy, but it's a crucial part of personal development. My experience with moving to a new city taught me that stepping into the unknown can bring unexpected joys and opportunities. By being open to new experiences, viewing change as an opportunity, and learning from past experiences, you can navigate life's changes with confidence and grace. Here's to accepting change and moving forward, ready to embrace whatever comes next.

NAVIGATING EDUCATION AS A QUEER STUDENT

High school: a time of awkward dances, questionable fashion choices, and trying to blend in with the crowd. For me, it was less "Saved by the Bell" and more "Nightmare on Elm Street." The hallways felt like a gauntlet, and fitting in was as elusive as a snowstorm in July. One day, in a moment of misguided hope for connection, I hinted at my queerness to a so-called friend during lunch. It was like dropping a match into a room full of fireworks. By the end of the day, the whispers had turned into a cacophony of judgmental stares. My sanctuary? The library, where I buried myself in books to escape the real-life horror show around me.

Navigating education as a queer student is more than just surviving the academic gauntlet. It's about finding your tribe, safeguarding your sanity, and sometimes, just making it through the day without wanting to disappear into the nearest supply closet. The challenge of juggling classes, social pressures, and the quest for self-acceptance is like playing a game of high-stakes dodgeball, where the balls are prejudice and ignorance. But in this game, the stakes are your mental health and sense of self-worth.

Practical Advice

1. **Find Your Tribe:** Look for teachers, counselors, or any school staff who give off that vibe of "I'm not a total bigot." They can be your lifeline in a sea of ignorance.

2. **Start or Join an LGBTQ+ Group:** If your school has a GSA or something similar, join it. If not, channel your inner rebel and start one. These groups can be the difference between feeling alone and finding a sense of belonging.

3. **Leverage Online Resources:** When your school feels like it's stuck in the 1950s, turn to the internet. There are countless forums, websites, and social media groups that can provide support, advice, and a sense of community.

4. **Balance Assertiveness with Safety:** Stand up for yourself, but don't be a martyr. Know when to fight back and when to keep your head down for self-preservation.

5. **Stay Focused on Your Goals:** Remember, you're in school to build a future. Use every slight and every sneer as fuel to drive you towards your goals.

Lesson #11

Navigating the educational system as a queer student is like playing a high-stakes game of dodgeball where the balls are prejudice and ignorance. It requires a mix of resilience, cunning, and a wicked sense of humor. Each step you take not only paves the way for your own future but also clears a path for those who will follow in your footsteps.

THE VALUE OF EDUCATION (FORMAL & INFORMAL)

Education. Sure, it's what you get in school, but it's also what you pick up in the real world, usually when you least expect it and often when you're making a mess of things. Let's dive into how both formal and informal education have shaped me, and why those impromptu life lessons can be just as vital as the ones learned inside a classroom.

In school, I was your typical overachiever. I studied hard, got good grades, and followed the rules. Formal education provided me with a solid foundation, teaching me essential skills like critical thinking, problem-solving, and surviving on coffee and adrenaline during finals week.

But honestly, some of the most impactful lessons came from outside those academic walls.

Take the time I decided to learn cooking. I had just moved out on my own, and I was determined to prove that I could survive without subsisting on ramen and takeout. My first attempt at making a proper meal was spaghetti Bolognese. Armed with a recipe and an unjustified amount of confidence, I dove in.

Things started to go south pretty quickly. I mistook a tablespoon for a teaspoon when adding chili flakes, setting my mouth on fire. Then, I managed to confuse sugar with salt—let's just say dessert-like pasta is not something you want to try. By the end of it, my kitchen looked like a war zone, and I was seriously considering never cooking again.

But then something clicked. Amidst the chaos, I realized I had learned more in those few disastrous hours than I had in years of being spoon-fed information. I learned to pay attention to details, to correct mistakes as I go, and most importantly, to laugh at myself when things go wrong. These lessons were invaluable and applied to so many areas of my life beyond cooking.

Practical Advice

1. **Seek Knowledge from Various Sources:** Don't limit your learning to traditional settings. Books, documentaries, online courses, and conversations with diverse people can all be rich sources of knowledge. Be curious and open-minded, and

seek out opportunities to learn from different perspectives.

2. **Apply Learning to Real-Life Situations:** The true value of education lies in its application. Whether it's a skill learned in a workshop or a concept from a book, find ways to incorporate your learning into daily life. Practical application not only reinforces what you've learned but also enhances your ability to adapt and innovate.

3. **Value Both Formal and Informal Education:** Recognize that education doesn't end with a diploma. Life itself is a continuous learning experience. Value the lessons learned from everyday experiences, jobs, hobbies, and interactions. These informal lessons often provide the practical wisdom that complements formal education.

Lesson #12

Education enriches life and broadens perspectives. My experiences in formal education laid a strong foundation, but the lessons learned outside the classroom have been equally transformative. By seeking knowledge from various sources, applying it to real-life situations, and valuing both formal and informal education, we can continue to grow and evolve throughout our lives. Here's to embracing education in all its forms and recognizing the lifelong journey of learning that shapes us into well-rounded, knowledgeable individuals.

CULTIVATING RESILIENCE

Resilience. It's like a muscle you never knew you had until life decides to drop a ton of bricks on you. Overcoming challenges and bouncing back from adversity isn't just a useful skill; it's the secret sauce of surviving adulthood with your sanity (mostly) intact.

Let's rewind to my early twenties, a time when I thought I had life all figured out. Spoiler alert: I didn't. I had just landed what I thought was my dream job, only to realize that dreams can sometimes be nightmares in disguise. The job was demanding, the boss was a tyrant, and the work environment was about as friendly as a pack of hyenas.

One particularly hellish day, my boss called me into his office to chew me out for something that wasn't even my fault. As he berated me, I felt my confidence crumble. Walking out of his office, I was ready to quit right there and then. But something inside me snapped, and not in the way you'd expect. I decided that this wasn't going to break me. Instead, I was going to use this experience as a stepping stone, not a stumbling block.

I started to develop a positive mindset, seeing every challenge as an opportunity to learn and grow. I treated setbacks like plot twists in a bad TV show—unexpected, annoying, but ultimately surmountable. When my boss continued to be unbearable, I didn't just sit there and take it. I looked for ways to improve my situation, from seeking mentorship within the company to exploring new career opportunities.

Eventually, I found a better job that valued my skills and respected me as a person. Looking back, that toxic job was the crucible that forged my resilience. It taught me that no matter how tough things get, I could bounce back stronger.

Practical Advice

1. **Develop a Positive Mindset:** It sounds cliché, but it works. Focus on the positives in any situation, no matter how bleak. Reframe challenges as opportunities to grow. Remember, even Batman had to deal with the Joker.

2. **Learn from Setbacks:** Setbacks are inevitable, but they're also invaluable learning experiences.

Analyze what went wrong, learn from it, and use that knowledge to avoid similar pitfalls in the future. It's like video game logic—each failure gets you closer to mastering the level.

3. **Stay Persistent and Determined:** Persistence is key. Keep pushing forward, even when it feels like you're moving through molasses. Determination will carry you through the rough patches and out the other side, stronger and wiser.

Lesson #13

Resilience is the key to overcoming challenges and achieving success. Life will throw curveballs, but it's how you respond that defines your journey. Developing a positive mindset, learning from setbacks, and staying persistent will help you bounce back from adversity and emerge stronger. So here's to cultivating resilience, tackling life's challenges head-on, and coming out the other side with a badass story to tell.

DEALING WITH PEER PRESSURE

Peer pressure. It's that sneaky force that can make you do things you never thought you would, just to fit in or avoid rocking the boat. Navigating the treacherous waters of peer pressure is a rite of passage, and it's one that often comes with some hard-earned lessons.

Let me take you back to my college days, when I was living with my grandparents in Arizona. They had an amazing house—complete with a pool, a cabana, and a backyard that looked like it was ripped straight out of a luxury magazine. One weekend, my grandparents decided to take a trip and left me in charge. Grandpa had one rule: no guests. Simple enough, right? Except I had friends who loved to test boundaries.

As soon as they heard about my temporary paradise, my friends started pushing me to throw a party. At first, I resisted. Grandpa's warning echoed in my mind, but the pressure kept mounting. "Come on, it'll be fun!" they said. "What's the worst that could happen?" Famous last words.

I caved. What started as a small gathering quickly turned into a rager. The pool and cabana were packed, the backyard was buzzing with people, and the house was filled to the brim. It was a scene straight out of a movie—one of those movies where everything goes disastrously wrong.

Amid the chaos, my best friend's purse was stolen. It wasn't just any purse; it contained her makeup and medicine. She was understandably upset and filed a police report for insurance purposes. We thought that would be the end of it, but then the story made it into the local newspaper. My grandpa read about it, and let's just say he was less than thrilled.

The aftermath was brutal. Grandpa's trust was shattered, and I had to face the music. It was a harsh lesson about the consequences of giving in to peer pressure and not respecting boundaries.

Practical Advice

1. **Stay True to Yourself:** Remember your values and priorities. Don't compromise them just to fit in. Peer pressure can be strong, but your sense of self should be stronger. Like they say, if your friends jumped off a bridge, would you?

2. **Choose Friends Who Respect Your Decisions:** Surround yourself with people who respect your choices and values. True friends won't pressure

you into doing something that makes you uncomfortable. They'll support you, even if you decide to sit out the latest crazy adventure.

3. **Practice Assertiveness:** Learn to say no confidently. It's a powerful word that can save you from a lot of regret. Practice being assertive in smaller situations so you're prepared to stand your ground when it really counts.

Lesson #14

Standing up to peer pressure builds character and integrity. It's not always easy, but resisting the urge to conform when it conflicts with your values is crucial. By staying true to yourself, choosing friends who respect your decisions, and practicing assertiveness, you can navigate the pressures of social conformity with grace and strength. Here's to making choices that align with who you truly are and not letting peer pressure steer your life off course.

THE ROLE OF MENTORS

Mentors. They're like the Yodas of our lives—wise, sometimes cryptic, but always there to guide us through the quagmire of our personal and professional journeys. A good mentor can make all the difference, turning confusion into clarity and obstacles into stepping stones.

I remember vividly the impact one particular mentor had on me. During my early years in the hospitality industry, I was working at a high-end restaurant, still finding my footing in a demanding and competitive field. Enter Stacy, the restaurant's general manager, a no-nonsense woman with a knack for turning chaos into order.

Stacy had this incredible ability to see potential where others saw only inexperience. She took me under her wing, teaching me everything from handling difficult customers to managing a team with grace under pressure. One night, the restaurant was slammed, and we were short-staffed. Orders were piling up, customers were getting impatient, and the kitchen was on the verge of mutiny. I was teetering on the edge of a meltdown.

Stacy stepped in, calm and collected. She didn't take over; instead, she guided me through the storm. "Focus on one thing at a time," she said, her voice steady. "Prioritize and communicate. You've got this." With her support, we navigated the chaos, and by the end of the night, the crisis had passed. It was a baptism by fire, and I came out stronger, more confident in my abilities.

From Stacy, I learned the value of composure under pressure and the importance of clear communication. She didn't just teach me how to run a restaurant; she taught me how to lead, how to inspire, and how to believe in myself. Her mentorship was a game-changer, and her lessons have stayed with me long after I moved on from that job.

Practical Advice

1. **Seek Out Mentors in Various Areas of Life:** Don't limit yourself to finding a mentor in just one field. Seek out mentors in different areas—career, personal development, hobbies. Each mentor can offer unique insights and guidance that enrich your life in different ways.

2. **Learn from Their Experiences and Wisdom:** Pay attention to the stories and lessons your mentors share. Their experiences are a goldmine of knowledge. Take notes, ask questions, and apply their wisdom to your own life. Mentors have walked paths you haven't yet, and their guidance can save you from many pitfalls.

3. **Give Back by Mentoring Others:** Once you've benefited from mentorship, pay it forward. Be a mentor to someone else. Sharing your knowledge and experience not only helps others but also reinforces your own learning. It's a rewarding cycle of growth and support.

Lesson #15

Mentors play a crucial role in personal and professional growth. They provide the guidance, support, and wisdom that help us navigate life's challenges and seize its opportunities. By seeking out mentors, learning from their experiences, and giving back through mentoring others, we create a network of growth and support that enriches our lives. Here's to the mentors who light our way and to becoming mentors ourselves, guiding the next generation with the lessons we've learned.

UNDERSTANDING & EMBRACING DIVERSITY

Diversity. It's not just a trendy buzzword but a vibrant reality that brings color and depth to our lives. As a white queer man, I've always felt a disconnect from the blandness of my white culture, which often seemed limited to crock pots, football, and church functions. Seeking a richer, more diverse tapestry of experiences, I immersed myself in different cultures at every opportunity.

Right after I graduated high school at 17, I left home and embarked on a journey to explore the world beyond my upbringing. First stop: Arizona. From there, I moved to Atlanta, then Florida, and finally Puerto Rico. Each place offered a unique blend of cultures and perspectives, teaching me more about the world and myself than I ever could have imagined.

In Arizona, I encountered a blend of Native American and Mexican cultures. The food, the traditions, the art—it was a sensory explosion compared to the monotony I had known. Moving to Atlanta, I was embraced by the vibrant African American community. The music, the history, and the resilience of the people there were profoundly inspiring.

Florida was a melting pot of cultures. I not only soaked up the Cuban influence, from the pulsating rhythms of salsa to the aromatic spices of Cuban cuisine, but I was also introduced to the richness of Judaism. I attended Shabbat dinners, learned about Jewish history and traditions, and was welcomed into a community that broadened my understanding of faith and cultural identity.

But it was in Puerto Rico that my immersion in diversity truly deepened. My husband, a proud Puerto Rican, opened my eyes to the rich tapestry of his people's history, culture, and food. Through him, I learned about the struggles and triumphs of Puerto Rico, from the resilience of its people in the face of hurricanes to the vibrant celebrations of its cultural heritage.

Living in Puerto Rico during a politically charged era only intensified my commitment to understanding and embracing diversity. The hateful rhetoric and divisive politics I saw around me fueled my desire to dig deeper into other cultures, to find common ground, and to celebrate our differences. I became actively involved in community events, cultural festivals, and advocacy groups, learning from people of all backgrounds and walks of life.

In these times, when hate and division are stoked by fear and ignorance, embracing diversity is not just an act of personal growth—it's a form of resistance. It's about standing up against the forces that seek to divide us and recognizing that our differences are what make us stronger. By learning about and celebrating the cultures and experiences of others, we build bridges instead of walls, fostering a society grounded in mutual respect and understanding.

Practical Advice

1. **Be Open-Minded and Curious:** Approach life with an open mind and genuine curiosity about others. Ask questions, listen to stories, and engage with people from different backgrounds. Curiosity can break down barriers and build bridges of understanding.

2. **Learn About Different Cultures and Perspectives:** Take the time to learn about cultures and perspectives different from your own. Read books, watch documentaries, attend cultural events, and travel if you can. Exposure to diverse viewpoints enriches your understanding of the world and helps dispel stereotypes.

3. **Promote Inclusivity in Your Community:** Actively promote inclusivity in your community. Support businesses owned by people from diverse backgrounds, advocate for inclusive policies at

work or in your neighborhood, and create spaces where everyone feels welcome and valued.

Lesson #16

Diversity is a strength that should be celebrated and respected. My journey from a homogeneous upbringing to a life rich in diverse experiences has taught me that embracing diversity enriches life in countless ways. Especially in these politically divisive times, learning about different cultures and perspectives is a powerful antidote to hate and ignorance. By being open-minded and curious, promoting inclusivity, and standing up for our shared humanity, we can create a more vibrant, respectful, and connected world. Here's to celebrating the beautiful mosaic of humanity and recognizing the strength that comes from our differences.

MANAGING FINANCES EARLY ON

Managing finances. It's one of those adulting skills that many of us wish we'd been taught in school, alongside how to do taxes and why student loans are basically legalized robbery. My journey with money has been a rollercoaster, full of early mistakes that served as brutal but necessary lessons.

Right after high school, when I was 17, I was all set to conquer the world—or so I thought. Moving to Arizona was my first taste of independence, and with that came my first taste of financial freedom. The problem? I had no idea what I was doing. My concept of budgeting was about as solid as a sandcastle at high tide.

Within months, I found myself in a financial mess. I got my first credit card and treated it like free money. Shopping sprees, dining out, and buying all the latest gadgets—why not? It was only when the bills started piling up that reality hit me like a freight train. I was in debt, my credit score was plummeting, and I had no idea how to dig myself out of this hole.

It took a major wake-up call to get my act together. One particularly embarrassing moment was when my card was declined at a grocery store checkout. As I awkwardly fumbled through my wallet, the cashier looked at me with a mix of pity and impatience. That's when I decided I needed to get serious about my finances.

I started by educating myself about personal finance. I devoured books, watched videos, and even took a few online courses. One of the best decisions I made was to create a budget and stick to it. It was painful at first, cutting back on luxuries and learning to differentiate between wants and needs. But gradually, I saw progress.

Another lifesaver was setting up automatic savings. Each month, a portion of my paycheck went straight into a savings account. At first, it wasn't much, but over time, it grew into a safety net that gave me peace of mind. I also tackled my credit card debt head-on, paying off the highest interest cards first and gradually working my way down.

Through discipline and a lot of trial and error, I managed to turn my financial situation around. These early mistakes taught me the importance of financial literacy and set the foundation for my future stability.

Practical Advice

1. **Budget and Save Regularly:** Create a budget that outlines your income, expenses, and savings goals. Track your spending and adjust as needed. Set up automatic transfers to your savings account to ensure you're consistently setting money aside.

2. **Educate Yourself About Personal Finance:** Take the time to learn about personal finance. Read books, take courses, and seek advice from financial experts. The more you know, the better equipped you'll be to make smart financial decisions.

3. **Make Informed Financial Decisions:** Before making any significant financial commitments, do your research. Understand the terms of any loans or credit cards, and always consider the long-term impact of your decisions. Don't be afraid to ask for help if you're unsure.

Lesson #17

Financial literacy is essential for long-term stability and success. Learning how to manage your finances early on can save you a lot of stress and hardship down the road. By budgeting and saving regularly, educating yourself about personal finance, and making informed decisions, you can build a solid financial foundation. Here's to making smart money moves and securing a stable, successful future.

THE IMPORTANCE OF DREAMING BIG

Dreaming big. It sounds like something straight out of a motivational poster, but the truth is, dreaming big can inspire growth and lead to achievements you never thought possible. It's about pushing the boundaries of what you think you can do and having the guts to chase those dreams with everything you've got.

Let me tell you about a dream that seemed impossible for a long time: writing a book and telling my story. For years, the idea of becoming an author was a distant fantasy. I was a bit of a mess, juggling various jobs, navigating life as a gay man, and trying to figure out where I fit in the world. My life was full of vibrant chaos, from wild nights out to intense personal struggles.

But amidst all the messiness, the dream of writing a book kept nagging at me. I wanted to share my experiences, the ups and downs, the lessons learned, and the journey of self-discovery. It wasn't just about telling my story; it was about healing myself and, hopefully, helping others in the process.

The first step was setting the ambitious goal: write a book. It felt daunting, like staring up at a mountain from its base. But I knew that if I didn't aim high, I'd never make it happen. So, I broke down this massive goal into smaller, manageable steps.

I started by journaling, pouring my thoughts and experiences onto paper. At first, it was just a therapeutic exercise, but gradually, those journal entries began to form the skeleton of a book. I read books on writing, attended workshops, and sought advice from other writers. Each step, no matter how small, was progress.

There were countless setbacks. Writing dredged up painful memories and insecurities. There were days when I questioned whether anyone would care about my story. But every time doubt crept in, I reminded myself why I started. I wanted to heal, to connect, and to share the raw, unfiltered truth of my journey.

Staying motivated was key. I set aside time each day to write, even if it was just a few sentences. I surrounded myself with supportive friends who believed in my dream and encouraged me to keep going. And slowly but surely, my messy past transformed into a coherent narrative.

Finally, after years of hard work, my book was complete. Holding the finished manuscript in my hands was surreal. It wasn't just about achieving a goal; it was about realizing my full potential and proving to myself that with enough determination, even the wildest dreams can come true.

Practical Advice

1. **Set Ambitious Goals:** Don't be afraid to dream big. Set goals that challenge you and push you out of your comfort zone. Ambitious goals inspire you to grow and strive for excellence.

2. **Break Them Down into Actionable Steps:** Once you have your big goal, break it down into smaller, manageable steps. Create a plan that outlines what you need to do to achieve each step. This makes the process less overwhelming and more achievable.

3. **Stay Motivated and Persistent:** Keep your eye on the prize and stay motivated, even when things get tough. Surround yourself with supportive people, celebrate small victories along the way, and remind yourself why you started. Persistence is key to overcoming obstacles and reaching your goals.

Lesson #18

Dreaming big leads to realizing your full potential. Writing my book was a journey of self-discovery and healing, proving that even the most daunting dreams can become reality with determination and hard work. By setting ambitious goals, breaking them down into actionable steps, and staying motivated and persistent, you can turn your dreams into reality. Here's to dreaming big and chasing those dreams with all your heart.

BALANCING AMBITION WITH SELF-CARE

mbition. It's the driving force that pushes us to achieve our goals and chase our dreams. But unchecked ambition can lead to burnout if we don't take time to refuel with self-care. Finding the balance between striving for success and taking care of ourselves is crucial for long-term well-being and productivity.

Let me take you back to a time when I was determined to make a name for myself as a leader in the hospitality industry. Detroit was experiencing a resurgence, and the downtown area was booming with new opportunities. I jumped at the chance to be at the forefront, opening new hotels and restaurants that would redefine the city's hospitality landscape.

I threw myself into the work with relentless enthusiasm. My days were filled with back-to-back meetings, overseeing construction projects, hiring staff, and planning grand openings. I wanted everything to be perfect, from the décor to the menu to the customer experience. I was driven by the vision of creating something extraordinary and leaving a lasting mark on Detroit's hospitality scene.

For a while, it was exhilarating. The sense of accomplishment was immense as I saw my projects come to life. The buzz of a new hotel opening or a restaurant launch was addictive. But as the months went by, the nonstop grind began to take its toll. I was working 16-hour days, barely sleeping, and neglecting my health. My diet consisted of whatever I could grab on the go, and exercise was a distant memory.

One particularly hectic month, I was juggling the grand opening of a new hotel and the launch of a high-end restaurant simultaneously. The pressure was intense, and I was running on fumes. I started to notice the signs of burnout—constant fatigue, irritability, and a creeping sense of dread every morning. But I pushed through, convincing myself that I just needed to get through the next big event.

It wasn't until I had a minor health scare that I realized I couldn't keep going at this pace. I was forced to take a step back and reevaluate my approach. My ambition was important, but so was my well-being. I had to find a way to balance both.

Practical Advice

1. **Prioritize Self-Care Activities:** Self-care isn't a luxury; it's a necessity. Schedule time for activities that rejuvenate you, whether it's exercise, meditation, reading, or simply taking a walk. Treat these activities as non-negotiable appointments with yourself.

2. **Set Boundaries to Avoid Burnout:** Learn to say no and set boundaries to protect your time and energy. This means not overcommitting and recognizing your limits. It's okay to decline additional work or social obligations if it means preserving your well-being.

3. **Make Time for Relaxation and Hobbies:** Balance work with leisure. Engage in hobbies that bring you joy and relaxation. Whether it's painting, cooking, gardening, or binge-watching your favorite series, make time for activities that allow you to unwind and recharge.

Lesson #19

A balanced life enhances productivity and well-being. My experience in Detroit's hospitality industry taught me that ambition must be tempered with self-care. By prioritizing self-care activities, setting boundaries, and making time for relaxation and hobbies, we can achieve our goals without sacrificing our health. Here's to finding the equilibrium between ambition and self-care, ensuring a fulfilling and sustainable journey towards success.

BUILDING LIFELONG FRIENDSHIPS

F riendships. They are the relationships we choose, the family we build outside of blood ties. Building and maintaining lifelong friendships is a journey filled with shared experiences, mutual growth, and the occasional bump in the road. But true friendships, the kind that last a lifetime, require effort, trust, and mutual respect.

Let me tell you about my best friend, Jennifer. We met when I was 14, a tumultuous time for any teenager, but especially for someone like me who felt out of place and often overlooked. Jennifer became the figure of love and consistency in my life when I needed it most. She mothered me and took care of me when no one else even noticed I was alone. She was my rock, my confidante, and my protector.

Our bond was solidified when I came out to her. It was one of the scariest moments of my life, but I knew I could trust her. Her response was nothing short of perfect. She hugged me tightly and said, "I've got your back, always." From that moment on, she became my fierce protector, ensuring that I felt safe and accepted. Her unwavering support gave me the courage to be myself.

Jennifer and I also shared a mutual love of Mariah Carey. Her music was the soundtrack of our teenage years, and we bonded over every high note and glittery performance. To this day, no matter where life takes us, we make it a point to attend Mariah's concerts together. Despite living on different sides of the globe now, we meet up, relive our younger days, and belt out our favorite Mariah hits at the top of our lungs.

Our friendship has weathered many storms. From the trials of adolescence to the challenges of adult life, Jennifer has always been there for me. During my toughest times, she has offered unwavering support and love. When I felt lost and overwhelmed, she reminded me of my worth and encouraged me to keep going.

Practical Advice

1. **Nurture Your Friendships:** Friendships, like any relationship, require effort to thrive. Make time for your friends, whether it's through regular meetups,

phone calls, or even just a quick text to check in. Show that you value and appreciate their presence in your life.

2. **Communicate Openly and Honestly:** Open and honest communication is key to any healthy relationship. Share your thoughts and feelings, and be willing to listen to your friends' perspectives. Address conflicts directly and with empathy, ensuring that misunderstandings don't grow into bigger issues.

3. **Be There for Each Other in Good Times and Bad:** True friends celebrate each other's successes and provide support during tough times. Be a reliable and consistent presence in your friends' lives, offering a shoulder to lean on when needed and sharing in their joy when things go well.

Lesson #20

Lifelong friendships are a source of joy, support, and growth. My journey with Jennifer taught me that true friendships require effort, trust, and mutual respect. By nurturing these relationships, communicating openly, and being there for each other through thick and thin, we can build friendships that stand the test of time. Here's to the friends who become our chosen family and the bonds that enrich our lives beyond measure.

FINDING YOUR PASSION

P assion. It's that elusive spark that can transform a mundane existence into a life filled with purpose and joy. Finding your passion is a journey that requires exploration, curiosity, and a willingness to take risks. But once you discover it, the rewards are immeasurable.

My journey to finding my passion was anything but straightforward. I spent much of my early adulthood dabbling in various jobs, from hospitality to being a makeup artist, always feeling like something was missing. I was good at what I did, but I never felt truly fulfilled. There was always a nagging feeling that I was meant for something more, something that would ignite that elusive spark.

One day, while cleaning out an old drawer, I stumbled upon a dusty notebook from my teenage years. Flipping through the pages, I found stories, poems, and random musings—remnants of a time when writing was my escape and my joy. I realized that somewhere along the way, I had abandoned this passion in pursuit of more "practical" endeavors.

Inspired by this rediscovery, I decided to give writing another shot. I started small, jotting down thoughts and ideas during my breaks at work. Gradually, those scribbles turned into short stories and blog posts. The more I wrote, the more I felt that long-lost spark reignite. Writing became my refuge, a way to express myself and connect with others on a deeper level.

The transformative moment came when I decided to write a book. It was an ambitious goal, and I had no idea where to start, but I was determined to see it through. The process was challenging and filled with self-doubt, but it was also incredibly rewarding. Every word I wrote brought me closer to a version of myself that I had long buried.

Practical Advice

1. **Explore Different Interests:** Don't be afraid to try new things. Take up hobbies, attend workshops, and immerse yourself in different activities. The more you explore, the more likely you are to stumble upon something that ignites your passion.

2. **Follow What Excites You:** Pay attention to what excites and energizes you. What activities make you lose track of time? What topics do you love to talk about? These are clues to your passion. Follow them, even if they seem impractical at first.

3. **Be Persistent in Pursuing Your Passion:** Once you find your passion, pursue it with persistence and dedication. There will be obstacles and moments of doubt, but don't give up. The journey may be challenging, but the fulfillment you'll find is worth every effort.

Lesson #21

Finding and pursuing your passion leads to a fulfilling life. Rediscovering my love for writing transformed my life in ways I never imagined. It brought me joy, purpose, and a deeper connection with myself and others. By exploring different interests, following what excites you, and being persistent, you can discover a passion that fills your life with meaning. Here's to finding that spark and letting it guide you to a life of fulfillment and joy.

THE IMPORTANCE OF NETWORKING

N etworking. It's often seen as a buzzword, a necessary evil in the professional world. But the truth is, networking is a powerful tool that can open doors to new opportunities and foster personal and career growth. It's about building genuine relationships that can lead to unexpected and significant career advancements.

Let me tell you about a pivotal time in my career when networking and establishing strong professional relationships made all the difference. I was the general manager at a steakhouse for a high profile Celebrity Chef, in downtown Detroit. It was a challenging role, but I was passionate about it and determined to make an impact.

The executive chef of the property was an incredibly talented but often flustered individual. He had a habit of lashing out under pressure, and one night, his frustration boiled over, and I found myself on the receiving end of his anger. He came at me with negativity that I knew I did not deserve.

In that moment, I decided to stand my ground. I told him calmly but firmly, "I have never come at you with that negativity. Do not do that to me." My words must have hit home because later that night, he sent me an email apologizing. He said my words had impacted him deeply and made him rethink his approach. That email marked a turning point in our relationship. From then on, there was mutual respect and a stronger bond between us.

As time went on, our working relationship flourished. He appreciated my honesty and the respect I showed him, and I valued his incredible culinary skills and dedication. This newfound mutual respect led to an unexpected opportunity. The executive chef was set to become the culinary director of a new hotel in Detroit, a highly anticipated project in the city's revitalization efforts.

Because of the trust and rapport we had built, he invited me to join him at the new Hotel to help open the property. This opportunity was a significant career advancement for me, allowing me to play a pivotal role in one of Detroit's most exciting new ventures.

Practical Advice

1. **Build Genuine Relationships:** Networking isn't just about exchanging business cards. Focus on building genuine relationships. Be authentic, show interest in others, and foster connections based on mutual respect and shared interests.

2. **Stay Connected and Engaged:** Networking doesn't end after the first meeting. Follow up regularly, stay in touch, and engage with your network. Share updates, ask for advice, and offer support. Consistent engagement keeps relationships strong and opens doors for future opportunities.

3. **Offer Value to Your Network:** Networking is a two-way street. Offer value to your connections by sharing useful information, providing support, or connecting them with other valuable contacts. When you contribute to others' success, you build a network that's willing to support you in return.

Lesson #22

Networking is a powerful tool for career and personal growth. My experience at the steakhouse and the hotel taught me that building genuine relationships and staying connected can lead to significant opportunities. By focusing on authentic connections, staying engaged, and offering value, you can create a network that supports and propels you forward. Here's to the power of networking and the doors it can open on your journey to success.

LEARNING FROM FAILURES

F ailures. They're the dreaded, inevitable detours on the road to success. While they might sting and knock you off your feet, failures are some of the most valuable learning experiences you'll ever encounter. They teach resilience, creativity, and perseverance. Let me tell you about a major failure that transformed my perspective and set me on a better path.

During my early days in the hospitality industry, I was given the opportunity to manage a high-profile event at one of the restaurants I worked for. It was a big deal—a chance to prove myself and showcase my abilities. I was eager to impress and perhaps a bit too confident in my capabilities.

The event planning started off well. I was meticulous about every detail, from the menu to the guest list. However, as the event approached, things started to unravel. A key supplier missed a crucial delivery, the weather forecast predicted storms for our outdoor setting, and the staff seemed unprepared despite my numerous briefings. In my rush to manage everything, I made a series of hasty decisions, hoping to patch things up.

On the day of the event, everything that could go wrong did. The food wasn't up to our usual standard, the seating arrangements got mixed up, and the rain turned the outdoor setting into a muddy mess. Guests were dissatisfied, and I felt the crushing weight of failure.

In the aftermath, I was devastated. I replayed every decision in my mind, questioning where it all went wrong. It was tempting to blame external factors—the unreliable supplier, the unpredictable weather—but deep down, I knew I had to take responsibility. It was a humbling experience.

Practical Advice

1. **Analyze What Went Wrong:** Instead of wallowing in self-pity, take a step back and analyze the failure objectively. What decisions led to the mistakes? What could have been done differently? This analysis is crucial for understanding and learning from your errors.

2. **Learn and Grow from Your Mistakes:** Use your failure as a learning opportunity. Identify the lessons it taught you and apply them to future endeavors. In my case, I learned the importance of

contingency planning, clear communication with the team, and not spreading myself too thin.

3. **Don't Fear Failure; Embrace It as Part of the Journey:** Failure is an inevitable part of any journey toward success. Embrace it rather than fear it. Each failure is a stepping stone that brings you closer to your goals. Remember that even the most successful people have faced numerous failures along the way.

Lesson #23

Learning from failures leads to growth and eventual success. My major event planning flop was a tough pill to swallow, but it taught me invaluable lessons about preparation, teamwork, and resilience. By analyzing what went wrong, learning from my mistakes, and embracing failure as part of the journey, I grew both personally and professionally. Here's to seeing failures not as setbacks, but as opportunities for growth and stepping stones to success.

DEVELOPING LEADERSHIP SKILLS

Leadership. It's more than just a title or a position of authority; it's about guiding, inspiring, and supporting others to achieve a common goal. Developing leadership skills is an ongoing process that requires empathy, vision, and effective communication. Let me share a story about my journey into a leadership role and the challenges I faced along the way.

I was thrust into a leadership position when I became the general manager at that steakhouse in downtown Detroit. It was a role that came with high expectations and immense pressure. The team was diverse and talented, but also headstrong and occasionally difficult to manage. I knew I had to prove myself as a leader who could bring out the best in everyone while steering the restaurant to success.

One of the biggest challenges I faced was learning how to work in a union environment. I had never managed a unionized staff before, and navigating the intricacies of union rules and regulations was a steep learning curve. The staff had strong opinions and weren't shy about voicing them, especially when it came to adhering to union agreements. Balancing the needs of the business with the rights and expectations of the union employees required a delicate touch.

Early on, I encountered resistance when trying to implement changes. Some staff members were skeptical of my intentions and wary of any disruptions to the established order. It became clear that to lead effectively, I needed to build trust and demonstrate that I respected the union's role in protecting workers' rights.

I started by leading by example. I showed up early, stayed late, and put in the hard work. I wasn't afraid to roll up my sleeves and get involved in every aspect of the restaurant, from the kitchen to the front of the house. My goal was to demonstrate that I was committed to our collective success and that I valued everyone's contributions. Imagine trying to be Captain Picard in a galaxy of unpredictable crew members—boldly leading where no one wanted to be led.

Another critical aspect of my leadership was listening to and supporting my team. I held regular meetings where everyone had a chance to voice their concerns and ideas.

One of the most impactful changes came from a suggestion by a junior chef about reorganizing the kitchen layout to improve efficiency. Implementing this idea not only boosted productivity but also showed the team that their input was valued.

Navigating union negotiations was particularly challenging. There were times when union representatives and I were at an impasse over work schedules and roles. I learned the importance of patience, negotiation, and finding common ground. One breakthrough moment came during a heated discussion about staffing levels. By listening to the concerns of the union reps and explaining the business's needs transparently, we were able to reach a compromise that satisfied both parties.

Through it all, we aimed for excellence, and our efforts were rewarded. We were certified by Forbes with 4 stars two years in a row. Achieving this required intense training and supervision of our policies and expectations. It was a testament to the hard work, dedication, and collaborative spirit of the entire team. Think of it as surviving the Hunger Games, but instead of getting a fancy trophy, you get stars that validate your existence in the brutal world of hospitality.

Practical Advice

1. **Lead by Example:** Demonstrate the behaviors and work ethic you expect from your team. Show them that you are willing to do the hard work alongside

them and that you are committed to the collective goals.

2. **Listen to and Support Your Team:** Create an environment where team members feel heard and valued. Encourage open communication and be receptive to feedback and suggestions. Support your team through challenges and celebrate their successes.

3. **Continuously Develop Your Leadership Skills:** Leadership is an ongoing learning process. Seek out opportunities for professional development, whether through courses, workshops, or mentorship. Stay adaptable and open to new ideas and approaches.

Lesson #24

Effective leadership inspires and drives success. My journey as a general manager taught me that true leadership requires empathy, vision, and effective communication. By leading by example, listening to and supporting your team, and continuously developing your leadership skills, you can create an environment where everyone thrives. Here's to the leaders who inspire us and the lessons that guide us on our leadership journeys.

WORK-LIFE BALANCE

Work-life balance. It's one of those things that everyone talks about but few truly master. Struggling to find that balance can be exhausting, but achieving it is crucial for our overall well-being.

Let me share a story about my battle with work-life balance while opening an elite steakhouse in downtown Detroit. This wasn't just any steakhouse—it had its own meat cooler in the basement, the fanciest fixtures, and touches that made the whole place feel like a scene straight out of Gatsby's time. Meals cost hundreds of dollars, and every detail was meticulously planned to create an unparalleled dining experience.

To get this place open, we worked around the clock. Most days, my team and I were putting in 12-16 hours, doing everything from hiring and training staff to cleaning and even helping with construction to meet tight deadlines. The pressure was immense, and the workload was relentless.

During this intense period, my personal life took a hit. My husband, who is the most important person in my life, began to feel isolated. I was so consumed with the demands of the steakhouse that I hardly had any time or energy left for him. It was a tough realization, and the guilt weighed heavily on me. The last thing I wanted was for him to feel neglected or unimportant.

Determined to find a solution, I started by setting clear boundaries between work and personal life. I made a rule that unless it was an absolute emergency, work stayed at work. No more answering emails at dinner or taking calls during family time. I communicated these boundaries to my team, ensuring they knew I trusted them to handle things in my absence.

Prioritizing time for family and relaxation was the next step. I scheduled weekly dinners with my husband and set aside time for hobbies we both enjoyed. These small changes made a significant difference in my overall well-being and strengthened our relationship.

Practicing self-discipline and time management was essential. I became more efficient at work, delegating tasks and focusing on what truly mattered. I learned to say no to unnecessary meetings and projects that didn't align with my goals. This newfound discipline allowed me to leave work on time and fully engage in my personal life.

Practical Advice

1. **Set Clear Boundaries Between Work and Personal Life:** Define specific times when work ends, and personal life begins. Communicate these boundaries to your colleagues and stick to them. Protecting your personal time is essential for maintaining balance.

2. **Prioritize Time for Family and Relaxation:** Schedule regular activities with family and friends, and make time for hobbies and relaxation. These moments recharge your batteries and strengthen your personal relationships.

3. **Practice Self-Discipline and Time Management:** Be efficient with your work time. Delegate tasks, focus on priorities, and avoid overcommitting. Effective time management allows you to be productive at work and present in your personal life.

Lesson #25

A balanced life enhances both professional and personal fulfillment. My struggle with work-life balance while opening the elite steakhouse taught me that setting boundaries, prioritizing personal time, and practicing self-discipline are key to achieving harmony. By making intentional changes, I was able to find a balance that improved my overall well-being and strengthened my relationships. Here's to pursuing a balanced life and finding joy in both our work and personal worlds.

THE POWER OF PERSISTENCE

Persistence. It's the secret ingredient that can turn a daunting long-term goal into a reality. It's about staying committed, pushing through setbacks, and celebrating the small victories along the way. Let me share a story about a long-term goal that required persistent effort to achieve: getting into nursing school.

For as long as I can remember, I had a vision of becoming a nurse. The idea of helping others and making a difference in people's lives was incredibly appealing. However, turning that dream into reality required more than just good intentions. It demanded hard work, sacrifice, and an unyielding commitment.

To bolster my nursing school application, I volunteered at a hospice company, seeking those extra points that would make my application stand out. At the same time, I juggled two jobs to pay my bills. My days were a blur of work, volunteering, and studying. I often found myself wondering if I would ever see the light at the end of the tunnel.

The hardest part of the journey was pharmacology. I failed the course twice. Each failure was a heavy blow, making me question my capabilities and my decision to pursue nursing. But I refused to give up. I hit the books harder, sought help from tutors, and finally, after what felt like an eternity, I passed the course.

Getting into nursing school was a triumph. But once I started, I quickly realized that the reality of nursing was far different from my expectations. Drawing blood, wiping asses—it wasn't exactly the Florence Nightingale fantasy I had envisioned. Despite my initial enthusiasm, I found myself increasingly disheartened.

However, not all aspects of the clinical experience were bad. I discovered that I had a surprising affinity for working in a dementia and Alzheimer's home. There was something deeply rewarding about providing comfort and care to patients who were often confused and frightened. But even this couldn't overshadow the growing realization that nursing, as a whole, wasn't for me.

Practical Advice

1. **Stay Committed to Your Goals:** Define your long-term goals clearly and stay committed to them.

Remind yourself why you started and keep your vision in sight, even when the going gets tough.

2. **Don't Give Up in the Face of Setbacks:** Setbacks are inevitable, but they're not the end of the road. View them as learning opportunities and stay determined to overcome them. Persistence is about getting up every time you're knocked down.

3. **Celebrate Small Victories Along the Way:** Acknowledge and celebrate the small victories on your journey. Each step forward, no matter how small, brings you closer to your goal. These celebrations fuel your motivation and remind you of the progress you're making.

Lesson #26

Persistence leads to success and personal growth. My journey to get into nursing school, despite its ultimate revelation, taught me that staying committed to your goals, pushing through setbacks, and celebrating small victories are essential. Even when the destination isn't what you expected, the journey itself can offer valuable lessons and foster personal growth. Here's to the power of persistence and the incredible things it can help you achieve, even if they lead you to unexpected places.

ADAPTING TO TECHNOLOGICAL CHANGES

I n the age of rapid technological advancement, keeping up with the times can feel like trying to teach your grandparents how to use TikTok. But staying relevant and competitive means embracing these changes, even if it feels like you're jumping on a speeding train. Here's a story about adapting to a major technological shift in the workplace.

A few years back, my workplace decided to replace our old, reliable (albeit clunky) paper-based system with a shiny new digital platform. The promise was to streamline operations, reduce errors, and enhance productivity. The reality was like trying to go from riding a bike to piloting a space shuttle overnight.

The initial training sessions were overwhelming, filled with technical jargon that made my head spin. My team and I were used to the old ways, and this new system felt like a foreign language. Morale dipped as frustration rose, and even I, someone who prides himself on being tech-savvy, found the transition challenging.

Determined to lead by example, I decided to dive headfirst into the digital abyss. I spent extra hours after work studying the manuals, watching tutorials, and calling tech support more times than I'd like to admit. I made it a point to stay updated with every new feature and update, ensuring I was ahead of the curve.

The real breakthrough came when I realized that our resistance to change was rooted in fear of the unknown. To combat this, I organized additional training sessions, breaking down the process into manageable steps and providing one-on-one support where needed. I encouraged everyone to ask questions and share their struggles, fostering a supportive learning environment.

Slowly but surely, we all began to adapt. The new system, once an intimidating hurdle, became an invaluable tool. It streamlined our operations, reduced errors, and indeed enhanced productivity. The initial investment in learning and adapting paid off tenfold.

Practical Advice

1. **Stay Updated with Technological Advancements:** Technology evolves rapidly, so it's crucial to keep up with the latest developments. Subscribe to industry newsletters, attend webinars, and read articles to stay informed about new tools and trends.

2. **Be Open to Learning New Skills:** Embrace a growth mindset and be willing to learn new skills. Take advantage of training programs, online courses, and workshops. Continuous learning keeps you adaptable and competitive in a rapidly changing environment.

3. **Use Technology to Enhance Productivity:** Identify how technology can streamline your workflow and improve efficiency. Whether it's project management software, communication tools, or data analytics, leverage technology to enhance productivity and drive innovation.

Lesson #27

Adapting to technology drives progress and innovation. My experience with implementing a new digital system at work taught me that embracing technological changes is crucial for staying relevant and competitive. By staying updated with advancements, being open to learning new skills, and using technology to enhance productivity, we can navigate the challenges of technological shifts and leverage them for growth. Embracing the future and the endless possibilities that technology brings is not just necessary—it's exciting.

THE VALUE OF CONTINUOUS LEARNING

Continuous learning. It's the secret sauce that keeps life interesting and us adaptable. Think of it as a never-ending quest for knowledge, much like Gandalf's journey through Middle-earth, but with fewer hobbits and more late-night Googling. Let me share how embracing lifelong learning has profoundly impacted both my personal and professional life.

When I first started my career, I thought I had it all figured out. I had the degrees, the skills, and a dash of arrogance that often comes with youth. But life has a way of humbling you, and I quickly realized that what I knew was just a drop in the ocean compared to what was out there. The turning point came when I decided to dive headfirst into continuous learning.

It all began with a random course I took on digital marketing. At the time, I was knee-deep in managing various projects, and the ever-evolving digital landscape felt like a foreign planet. The course opened my eyes to new strategies and tools that I could apply immediately. The impact was immediate and transformative. Not only did it boost my professional capabilities, but it also ignited a passion for learning that I hadn't felt since my school days.

From there, my thirst for knowledge only grew. I started attending workshops, reading voraciously, and diving into subjects I was curious about but had never explored. Whether it was the latest advancements in technology or ancient history, I soaked it all in. Each new piece of knowledge was like adding another tool to my Swiss Army knife of life.

One of the most profound experiences came from a leadership workshop I attended. The skills and insights I gained there were like a revelation. I began to see my role differently, approaching challenges with a fresh perspective and newfound confidence. It wasn't just about managing people; it was about inspiring and empowering them. The workshop didn't just make me a better leader; it made me a better person.

Practical Advice

1. **Take Courses and Attend Workshops:** Invest in yourself by taking courses and attending workshops related to your interests and career. There's always something new to learn, and these opportunities provide structured environments to gain valuable knowledge.

2. **Read Books and Stay Curious:** Cultivate a habit of reading. Books are treasure troves of knowledge, whether they're fiction, non-fiction, or technical manuals. Stay curious about the world around you and let your interests guide your learning journey.

3. **Apply New Knowledge to Real-Life Situations:** Knowledge is only as good as its application. Take what you learn and put it into practice. Whether it's a new technique at work or a life hack at home, applying new knowledge reinforces learning and makes it more meaningful.

Lesson #28

Lifelong learning enriches life and expands opportunities. Embracing continuous learning has kept me adaptable, knowledgeable, and ever-evolving. By taking courses, staying curious, and applying new knowledge, we can navigate the complexities of life with confidence and creativity.

Here's to the endless journey of learning and the countless doors it opens along the way.

SETTING & ACHIEVING GOALS

Goals—they're like the North Star guiding us through the chaos of life. Without them, we'd be drifting like a lost Amazon package. With them, we become unstoppable forces of nature.

A few years back, I decided to take on a challenge that seemed as ridiculous as it was ambitious: running a marathon. Now, if you know me, you'd know my idea of exercise was more about lifting a wine glass than lifting weights. The idea of running 26.2 miles seemed as far-fetched as understanding quantum mechanics. But I wanted to push my limits and see what I was capable of. So, I set the goal: run a marathon within a year.

To start, I needed to make this goal specific and achievable. Running a marathon wasn't just about enduring the race; it was about training, building endurance, and not keeling over in the process. I found a beginner's training program and laid out my runs week by week. Each week's schedule was a mini-goal contributing to the larger one.

I began with small, manageable runs. Picture me trying to channel my inner Forrest Gump but ending up more like a wheezing walrus. I started with a mile or two, gradually increasing the distance each week. There were days when I felt like I could outrun the Flash, and days when I seriously considered burning my running shoes. But each run, no matter how short, was a step closer to my goal.

Tracking progress was crucial. I kept a running journal, noting distances, times, and how close I was to collapsing. This helped me see improvements over time and adjust my training as needed. When a knee injury reared its ugly head, I sought out a physiotherapist and tweaked my regimen to include more strength training and stretching.

A key part of achieving this goal was the support system I built around me. Friends and family cheered me on, and I joined a local running group for extra motivation. Sharing my goal with others made me accountable and provided a network of encouragement. It was like having my own personal fan club, minus the autographs.

After months of training, setbacks, and small victories, race day finally arrived. The marathon itself was grueling—26.2 miles of questioning my sanity. But crossing that finish line was one of the most exhilarating experiences of my life. The sense of accomplishment was overwhelming, proving the power of setting clear goals and relentlessly pursuing them.

Practical Advice

1. **Set Specific, Achievable Goals:** Define your goals clearly. Make them SMART: Specific, Measurable, Achievable, Relevant, and Time-bound. This clarity will help you focus your efforts and track your progress.

2. **Break Them Down into Manageable Steps:** Large goals can be intimidating. Break them into smaller, manageable tasks. Each small step forward is progress, and these incremental achievements keep you motivated.

3. **Track Progress and Adjust as Needed:** Keep a record of your progress. Whether it's through a journal, an app, or a spreadsheet, tracking your progress helps you stay on course and make necessary adjustments.

Lesson #29

Achieving goals brings a sense of accomplishment and direction. My marathon journey taught me the value of setting clear, specific goals and breaking them down into manageable steps. By tracking progress and staying adaptable, you can overcome obstacles and reach your objectives. Celebrating the incredible sense of achievement when you cross your own finish line is worth every step.

THE ROLE OF GRATITUDE IN SUCCESS

Gratitude—it's the secret sauce that transforms a mundane meal into a feast. Practicing gratitude isn't just about saying "thank you"; it's about cultivating a mindset that can change your outlook on life and pave the way for success.

Let's rewind to a particularly rough patch in my life. I was juggling multiple jobs, dealing with personal setbacks, and feeling like the universe had it out for me. My default setting became a blend of frustration and self-pity, and let's just say, it wasn't winning me any "Most Pleasant Person to Be Around" awards.

One day, a friend suggested I start a gratitude journal. My initial reaction? Eye roll. But, desperate times call for desperate measures, so I decided to give it a shot. Every night, I wrote down three things I was grateful for. They started small: a decent cup of coffee, finding a parking spot on the first try, a funny meme that made me laugh. Over time, I noticed a shift. My perspective began to change. Instead of focusing on everything that was going wrong, I started to see what was going right.

This small practice of gratitude had a ripple effect. My mood improved, my interactions with others became more positive, and I found myself handling stress with more grace. The more I focused on the positives, the more positives seemed to come my way. It was like flipping a switch in my brain—from a constant state of "Why me?" to "What's next?"

Expressing appreciation became a regular part of my routine. I made it a point to thank my colleagues for their hard work, acknowledge my friends for their support, and even appreciate the small acts of kindness from strangers. This practice didn't just make others feel good; it created a positive feedback loop that boosted my own morale and productivity.

One of the most significant transformations happened at work. By focusing on gratitude, I found myself more motivated and engaged. I started to see challenges as opportunities rather than obstacles. This shift in mindset not only improved my performance but also caught the attention of my superiors. Gratitude had literally changed my trajectory, paving the way for new opportunities and successes.

Practical Advice

1. **Keep a Gratitude Journal:** Each day, write down three things you are grateful for. They can be big or small, profound or trivial. The key is to make it a daily habit. This practice helps shift your focus from what's lacking to what's abundant in your life.

2. **Express Appreciation Regularly:** Make it a point to thank people around you. Whether it's a colleague for their hard work, a friend for their support, or even a stranger for a small act of kindness, expressing appreciation fosters positive relationships and creates a supportive environment.

3. **Focus on the Positives in Life:** Train your mind to look for the good in every situation. When faced with challenges, try to identify at least one positive aspect. This doesn't mean ignoring problems, but rather balancing them with a positive perspective.

Lesson #30

Gratitude enhances well-being and paves the way for success. My journey with gratitude taught me that focusing on the positives and expressing appreciation can transform your outlook and open doors to new opportunities. By keeping a gratitude journal, expressing appreciation regularly, and focusing on the positives in life, you can cultivate a mindset that attracts success and enriches your overall well-being. Here's to the power of gratitude and the incredible impact it can have on your life.

THE IMPORTANCE OF EMPATHY

E mpathy—it's the magic ingredient that keeps us from devolving into self-absorbed hermits. Imagine if everyone actually tried to understand each other instead of just shouting their opinions. Sounds idyllic, right? Well, here's a story of how empathy saved a friendship and reminded me why it's crucial to be a decent human being.

So, there I was at a dinner party that spiraled out of control. It was one of those nights where the wine was flowing, the conversation got heated, and suddenly, I found myself in a full-blown argument with a close friend. And the topic? Something as ridiculous as the correct way to make guacamole. Yeah, it got that intense.

My friend and I were stubbornly defending our avocado-mashing methods, and before we knew it, the debate escalated. The atmosphere turned icy, and we both left feeling angry and misunderstood. For days, I replayed the argument in my head, thinking about all the cutting comebacks I could have made.

Then, a realization hit me: what if I stopped trying to be right and started trying to understand my friend's perspective? Maybe there was more to their outburst than just a culinary disagreement. Swallowing my pride, I decided to reach out.

Instead of diving back into the argument, I asked my friend how they were really doing. And boy, did I get an earful. They'd been dealing with a mountain of stress—work issues, family drama, the works. The guacamole showdown was just the straw that broke the camel's back.

I listened—really listened—to their struggles. As they spoke, my irritation faded, replaced by genuine concern and empathy. I apologized for my part in the spat, not because I suddenly thought their guacamole recipe was superior, but because I understood why they had been so on edge.

That conversation didn't just mend our friendship; it strengthened it. We both left feeling heard, understood, and valued. Empathy had turned a potential friendship-ending conflict into a deeper bond.

Practical Advice

1. **Practice Active Listening:** Give the speaker your full attention. Don't plan your next argument while they're talking. Listen to understand, not to reply. This shows you value their perspective and fosters a genuine connection.

2. **Put Yourself in Others' Shoes:** Try to see the situation from their viewpoint. What might they be going through that's influencing their behavior? This deeper understanding helps you react with compassion instead of judgment.

3. **Show Compassion and Understanding:** Even if you don't agree with their viewpoint, acknowledge their feelings. A simple "I get why you'd feel that way" can defuse tension and build rapport.

Lesson #31

Empathy strengthens relationships and fosters harmony. The guacamole debacle taught me that empathy isn't just a feel-good buzzword—it's essential for resolving conflicts and deepening connections. By practicing active listening, putting ourselves in others' shoes, and showing compassion, we can transform our interactions and build stronger, more meaningful relationships. Here's to the power

of empathy and the difference it can make in our
lives.

KEEPING ROMANCE SPICY & ALIVE IN YOUR RELATIONSHIP

Keeping the romance alive in a long-term relationship is like tending to a bonfire—you need to keep feeding it the right fuel or it'll fizzle out and leave you in the cold. Without some effort, the spark can fade faster than a cheap lightbulb. But with a little creativity and a healthy dose of playfulness, you can keep the passion alive and ensure that your relationship remains hotter than a Netflix binge session.

One surefire way to keep things spicy is through surprise and spontaneity. Forget those predictable date nights; I'm talking about planning something unexpected that'll make your partner's jaw drop. Think along the lines of an impromptu road trip, a surprise concert, or a midnight picnic under the stars. Even a spontaneous dance-off in your living room can bring back that spark. Remember, the goal is to break the routine and show that you're still capable of sweeping them off their feet.

Another essential ingredient is maintaining physical affection. And no, I don't mean just the occasional peck on the cheek. Keep the fire burning with regular doses of hugs, kisses, and yes, those steamy make-out sessions that can turn into something more. Never underestimate the power of a well-timed butt grab or a playful tickle fight to keep things exciting.

Communication is also crucial. And I'm not talking about the "How was your day?" kind of chat. Dive into those deep conversations about your fantasies, your dreams, and what turns you on. Discuss those raunchy daydreams and share what makes you feel loved and desired. This kind of honesty can lead to some pretty electrifying revelations and help you understand each other on a more intimate level.

Don't forget to try new things together. Whether it's signing up for a salsa dancing class, trying out a new adventurous recipe, or exploring a new city, shared experiences create memories and keep the relationship exciting. And if you're really looking to spice things up, maybe venture into a new territory in the bedroom—

consent and communication are key, but exploring together can be a thrilling journey.

Laughter is your best friend when it comes to keeping romance alive. Humor is a powerful aphrodisiac. Watch a raunchy comedy, share those ridiculous memes, or just be goofy together. Laughter not only brings joy but also makes the tough times easier to handle. Plus, there's nothing quite like the bond created by an inside joke that makes you both burst out laughing at the most inappropriate times.

Lastly, never stop learning about each other. People change, and what worked five years ago might need a refresh. Stay curious about your partner's evolving tastes, interests, and fantasies. Ask questions, pay attention, and show genuine interest in what makes them tick. This ongoing discovery process keeps the relationship dynamic and ensures that you stay deeply connected.

Practical Advice

1. **Plan Surprises and Be Spontaneous:** Keep your partner on their toes with unexpected dates, gifts, or adventures. Small surprises can reignite the spark and show your partner that you care.

2. **Maintain Physical Affection:** Hold hands, kiss, and make time for intimacy. Physical connection is crucial for keeping the romance alive. Don't be shy about showing affection in playful and passionate ways.

3. **Communicate Openly:** Talk about your desires, fantasies, and what makes you feel loved. Honest dialogue can deepen your connection and ensure that both partners feel fulfilled.

4. **Try New Things Together:** Explore new hobbies, take classes, or go on adventures. Shared experiences create new memories and bring excitement to your relationship. And remember, a little adventure in the bedroom can go a long way.

5. **Laugh Together:** Humor is a powerful aphrodisiac. Watch funny movies, share jokes, and be playful. Laughter strengthens your bond and keeps the mood light, even when life gets tough.

6. **Stay Curious About Each Other:** Continuously learn about your partner. Ask questions, listen actively, and show interest in their thoughts and feelings. This ongoing discovery can keep the romance alive.

Lesson #32

A healthy romantic relationship enhances life and personal growth. Keeping the romance spicy and alive requires effort, creativity, and a willingness to explore new facets of your relationship. By planning surprises, maintaining physical affection, communicating openly, trying new things together, laughing, and staying curious about each other, you can ensure that your relationship remains vibrant and exciting. Here's to the magic of love, the spice of romance, and the joy of keeping the flame burning bright.

THE ART OF SAYING NO

Learning to say "no"—it's a life skill that can save you from a mountain of unnecessary stress and obligation. Contrary to popular belief, saying no isn't about being selfish; it's about setting boundaries and preserving your sanity.

Let's rewind to a time when I was the poster child for overcommitment. My calendar looked like a Jackson Pollock painting—an absolute mess of colors, appointments, and deadlines. I was saying yes to everything: work projects, social events, even that dreaded neighborhood committee.

I thought I was being helpful and indispensable. In reality, I was on the fast track to burnout.

One day, I hit rock bottom. It was a Wednesday, and I found myself double-booked for a work presentation and a friend's surprise birthday party. I had to choose between my career and my personal life. Spoiler alert: I bombed the presentation and missed the cake. That's when it hit me—I needed to learn the art of saying no.

I started small. The next time a colleague asked me to take on an extra project, I politely declined, citing my current workload. The world didn't end. My colleague understood and respected my honesty. Emboldened by this small victory, I began to set clearer boundaries.

Saying no wasn't just about declining work requests. It extended to social engagements and personal favors. I realized that my time was valuable and that I needed to prioritize what mattered most. Instead of attending every event, I chose quality over quantity, investing my time in activities and people that brought me joy and fulfillment.

One of the biggest lessons was learning that it's okay to disappoint people occasionally. You can't please everyone, and trying to do so only leads to resentment and exhaustion. I found that true friends and supportive colleagues appreciated my honesty and respected my boundaries.

Practical Advice

1. **Start Small:** Practice saying no to minor requests. This will build your confidence and help you understand that it's okay to prioritize your needs.

2. **Be Honest and Polite:** When declining, be honest about your reasons without over-explaining. A simple, "I'm sorry, I can't take this on right now," is often enough.

3. **Set Clear Boundaries:** Communicate your limits clearly and stick to them. Let people know when you're available and when you're not, and be consistent in enforcing these boundaries.

Lesson #33

Mastering the art of saying no can transform your life. By setting clear boundaries and prioritizing what truly matters, you protect your time and energy for the things that bring you joy and fulfillment. Remember, saying no isn't about being selfish—it's about valuing yourself enough to know your limits. Here's to reclaiming your time, one "no" at a time.

MANAGING LIFE'S TRANSITIONS

L ife transitions—they're like plot twists in the never-ending drama series of our lives. Whether it's changing careers, moving to a new place, or taking a leap of faith in any other aspect of life, managing these transitions with grace can lead to tremendous growth and resilience.

A few years ago, I decided to leave the hospitality industry and dive headfirst into the world of writing. It was a huge shift, and let's just say the transition wasn't exactly smooth sailing. I went from the structured chaos of managing restaurants to the quieter, yet equally demanding, life of a writer. My husband, my rock, was there to support me through it all, but the change was still a lot to handle.

At first, the lack of a structured routine was disorienting. I went from constantly interacting with people to spending long hours alone, staring at a blank screen. The isolation and uncertainty were daunting, but I knew this was the path I wanted to take. Staying flexible and open-minded was crucial. My grand plan of writing a best-selling novel right away didn't pan out, but I embraced the journey and the process. I started by setting smaller, achievable goals, like writing a certain number of pages each day or completing short stories. Each small success built my confidence and kept me moving forward.

Having my husband's support made a world of difference. On days when self-doubt crept in, he was there to remind me why I chose this path and to encourage me to keep going. We had many late-night conversations where he listened to my fears and helped me brainstorm ideas. His unwavering belief in me was the anchor I needed during this turbulent time.

Focusing on the positive aspects of change also helped. While the transition was challenging, it brought new opportunities and experiences. I discovered a passion for storytelling that I hadn't fully explored before. The freedom to create and the satisfaction of seeing my ideas come to life on the page were incredibly fulfilling.

Practical Advice

1. **Stay Flexible and Open-Minded:** Life rarely goes as planned. Embrace the unexpected and be

willing to adapt. Flexibility can turn potential setbacks into opportunities for growth.

2. **Lean on Your Support System:** Whether it's a partner, friends, or a supportive community, having people to lean on makes a big difference. Don't be afraid to ask for help and share your journey with those who care about you.

3. **Focus on the Positive Aspects of Change:** Change can be intimidating, but it also brings new opportunities. Focus on the positives and celebrate small victories to maintain a positive outlook.

Lesson #34

Embracing transitions fosters resilience and personal growth. My journey from the hustle and bustle of the hospitality industry to the solitary, creative world of writing taught me the importance of staying flexible, leaning on my support system, and focusing on the positives. By managing life's changes with grace and a touch of humor, we can turn challenges into opportunities and come out stronger on the other side. Here's to navigating life's plot twists and finding joy in the journey.

THE ROLE OF COMMUNITY AND GIVING BACK

Community—it's the lifeline that catches you in times of despair and lifts you when you need it most. Being part of a community and giving back isn't just about altruism; it's about finding a sense of belonging and purpose, especially during life's most challenging moments.

In the fall of 2017, my husband and I were in the final stages of planning our wedding. Our big day was set in Michigan, but Hurricane Maria had just swept through

Puerto Rico like an unwelcome guest, leaving a trail of devastation. The storm made it impossible for most of his family to leave the island and join us for the celebration. To add insult to injury, Trump's grand gesture of help was chucking paper towels into the crowd like he was at a sporting event. Thanks, but no thanks.

The hurricane's impact didn't just stop at our wedding; it sent shockwaves through our lives in the weeks and months that followed. My husband's family was thrown into chaos, grappling with power outages, food and water shortages, and the Herculean task of rebuilding. Tragically, his abuela passed away shortly after our wedding because she couldn't get the medical care she desperately needed.

Despite these hardships, the community of Puerto Rico showed an incredible spirit of resilience. Neighbors banded together to clear debris, shared their limited resources, and supported each other through one of the toughest times they'd ever faced. Watching this unfold from afar, we were both humbled and inspired by their strength and solidarity.

Back in Michigan, we knew we had to do something. We managed to get my husband's mother out of Puerto Rico and bring her to stay with us. After a harrowing journey, she arrived safely in Detroit. To raise awareness about the dire situation in Puerto Rico, my husband and his mother participated in a local news interview. They spoke about the island's devastation, the ongoing struggles, and the urgent need for aid and support.

This experience reinforced the importance of community and giving back. Seeing the people of Puerto Rico support each other through such a difficult time was a powerful reminder of the strength and resilience that comes from being part of a united community. It also highlighted how critical it is to extend help and raise awareness beyond our immediate circles.

Back in Detroit, we continued to support the relief efforts in any way we could, from organizing fundraisers to sending supplies to the island. It was our way of giving back and showing solidarity with those who had lost so much.

Practical Advice

1. **Get Involved in Community Activities:** Attend local events, join neighborhood groups, and participate in community projects. Getting involved helps you build connections and make a positive impact.

2. **Offer Your Time and Skills to Help Others:** Volunteer your time and use your skills to benefit others. Whether it's helping with relief efforts, organizing charity events, or supporting local initiatives, every bit of effort counts.

3. **Build Strong Connections Within Your Community:** Take the time to get to know your neighbors and build meaningful relationships. Strong connections create a support system that enriches your life and strengthens the community.

Lesson #35

Giving back enriches your life and strengthens the community. The aftermath of Hurricane Maria taught me the immense value of community support and the profound impact of giving back. By getting involved, offering your time and skills, and building strong connections, you create a sense of belonging and purpose that benefits everyone. Here's to the power of community, the strength of solidarity, and the fulfillment that comes from being part of something greater than ourselves. And maybe next time, we'll aim for more than just paper towels.

PRACTICING MINDFULNESS & MEDITATION

indfulness and meditation—sounds like something out of a Gwyneth Paltrow wellness guide, right? But before you roll your eyes and close this book, hear me out. These practices aren't just for the yoga gurus and the incense-burning crowd. They're for anyone who's ever felt like their brain is a browser with too many tabs open. Spoiler alert: that's all of us.

So, let's dive in without all the woo-woo. Mindfulness and meditation are like mental floss for your brain—essential for clearing out the gunk and keeping things running smoothly. Here's why they matter and how you can incorporate them into your daily chaos.

Our lives are a nonstop barrage of notifications, deadlines, and existential dread. Mindfulness and meditation offer a way to hit the pause button on the madness. They help you step back, take a deep breath, and reconnect with the present moment—because let's be real, most of us are either dwelling on the past or freaking out about the future.

Mindfulness is all about paying attention to the here and now without judgment. It's about noticing your thoughts, feelings, and surroundings without spiraling into an anxiety-fueled meltdown. Meditation, on the other hand, is like a workout for your brain. It involves focusing on a particular thought, object, or activity to train your attention and awareness.

Practical Advice

1. **Set Aside Time for Daily Meditation:**
   Start small. We're talking five minutes here, not an hour-long session where you chant and levitate. Find a quiet spot, sit comfortably, and focus on your breath. When your mind inevitably wanders to what's for dinner or that embarrassing thing you said five years ago, gently bring it back to your breath.

2. **Practice Mindfulness in Everyday Activities:**
   You don't need a meditation cushion to practice mindfulness. Try it while eating, walking, or even

145

washing dishes. Pay attention to the sensations, smells, and sounds. Engage fully in the activity without letting your mind drift to your to-do list or the latest Netflix drama.

3. **Use Mindfulness Techniques to Manage Stress:** Stress happens. When it does, take a few moments to focus on your breath. Deep, slow breathing can help calm your frazzled nerves. Try a body scan: start from your toes and move up to your head, noticing any tension and consciously relaxing those muscles. Remember, you're not auditioning for a zen master— just trying to keep your cool.

Benefits of Mindfulness and Meditation

- **Reduced Stress:** These practices help lower cortisol levels, aka the stress hormone. So, you can stop feeling like a caffeine-addicted squirrel all the time.

- **Improved Focus:** Training your mind to stay in the present boosts concentration and cognitive function. Think of it as upgrading your mental operating system.

- **Emotional Regulation:** Mindfulness helps you become more aware of your emotions, allowing you to respond thoughtfully rather than react

impulsively. Basically, you stop acting like a
toddler who missed nap time.

- **Enhanced Well-Being:** These practices promote
  a sense of inner peace and happiness. It's like
  finding the chill pill we all desperately need.

Lesson #36

Mindfulness and meditation lead to a peaceful and
centered life. Incorporating these practices into your
daily routine can drastically improve your mental and
emotional well-being. By setting aside time for daily
meditation, practicing mindfulness in everyday
activities, and using mindfulness techniques to
manage stress, you can navigate life's chaos with
more grace and less grumpiness. So, give it a try.
Your brain—and everyone who has to deal with you—
will thank you.

HEALTH & WELLNESS

L et's talk about health and wellness—a topic that can either make you feel like a fitness guru or a couch potato in denial. Prioritizing health and wellness is more than just hitting the gym once in a blue moon or choosing the salad over fries. It's about creating sustainable habits that keep you feeling good, both physically and mentally, so you can actually enjoy this crazy ride called life.

Imagine trying to navigate life without taking care of your health. It's like driving a car without ever getting an oil change or refilling the gas—eventually, you're going to break down. Prioritizing your health and wellness is essential for maintaining the energy, strength, and mental clarity you need to tackle whatever life throws your way.

Practical Advice

1. Maintain a Balanced Diet and Exercise Regularly:

- *Balanced Diet*: No, you don't have to swear off all your favorite foods and survive on kale smoothies. It's about moderation and variety. Aim for a diet rich in fruits, vegetables, lean proteins, and whole grains. And yes, you can still have that slice of pizza —just not the whole pie.

- *Exercise:* Find an activity you enjoy so working out doesn't feel like a chore. Whether it's dancing, hiking, swimming, or even a brisk walk around the neighborhood, the key is to stay active. Aim for at least 150 minutes of moderate exercise per week. Your body (and your mood) will thank you.

2. Get Regular Health Check-Ups:

Don't wait until something goes wrong to see a doctor. Regular check-ups can catch potential issues before they become serious. Think of it as routine maintenance for your body. Schedule annual physicals, keep up with vaccinations, and don't ignore those mysterious aches and pains.

3. Practice Self-Care and Stress Management:

- **Self-Care:** It's not just about bubble baths and face masks (though those are nice too). Self-care includes anything that helps you recharge—reading, meditating, spending time with loved ones, or even binge-watching your favorite show guilt-free.

- **Stress Management:** Life is stressful, but how you manage that stress makes all the difference. Practice mindfulness, deep breathing exercises, or yoga. Find what works for you to keep your stress levels in check. And remember, it's okay to ask for help when you need it.

Lesson #37

Health and wellness are the foundation of a fulfilling life. By maintaining a balanced diet, exercising regularly, getting regular health check-ups, and practicing self-care and stress management, you're investing in yourself. This investment pays off in the form of more energy, better mental clarity, and an overall sense of well-being. So, take care of yourself— you're the only you we've got. Here's to a healthier, happier life!

THE JOY OF TRAVEL & EXPLORATION

Travel and exploration—these are pursuits that pull you out of your everyday routine and thrust you into a world of new experiences. It's more than just ticking off places on a bucket list or collecting Instagram-worthy photos. Travel is about discovering new perspectives, embracing different cultures, and ultimately, enriching your life in countless ways.

Travel broadens your horizons, challenges your assumptions, and provides a fresh lens through which to view the world. It's about stepping into the unknown and allowing yourself to be transformed by the people you meet, the cultures you encounter, and the landscapes you traverse. Exploration, whether near or far, can ignite a sense of wonder and curiosity that stays with you long after the journey ends.

Practical Advice

1. Plan Trips to New Places:
Whether it's a weekend road trip or an international adventure, make it a priority to explore new destinations. Research your chosen location, plan your itinerary, but also leave room for spontaneity. Some of the best travel experiences come from unplanned detours and unexpected discoveries.

2. Be Open to New Cultures and Experiences:
Traveling isn't just about sightseeing; it's about immersing yourself in different cultures. Try local foods, participate in cultural traditions, and engage with the locals. Approach each new experience with an open mind and a willingness to learn. This openness can lead to profound insights and meaningful connections.

3. Take Time to Explore Your Surroundings:
You don't always need to travel far to experience the joys of exploration. Take the time to discover your own city or nearby areas. Visit local museums, parks, historical sites, and neighborhoods you've never been to before. Often, there are hidden gems close

to home that offer rich experiences and new perspectives.

Benefits of Travel and Exploration

- **Broadens Perspectives:** Traveling exposes you to different ways of life, helping you understand and appreciate cultural diversity. It challenges your preconceived notions and encourages empathy and open-mindedness.

- **Enhances Personal Growth:** By stepping out of your comfort zone, you develop resilience, adaptability, and problem-solving skills. Travel experiences can boost your confidence and inspire creativity.

- **Creates Lasting Memories:** The adventures you embark on and the people you meet along the way create lasting memories. These experiences often become cherished stories that you'll reminisce about for years to come.

Lesson #38

Travel and exploration bring joy and personal growth. They teach us to see the world through different lenses and appreciate the diversity that makes life so vibrant. By planning trips to new places, being open to new cultures and experiences, and taking time to explore our surroundings, we can enrich our lives in ways we never imagined. So, pack your bags (or just grab your walking shoes) and get ready for an adventure. The world is waiting for you, and there's so much to discover.

FINDING PEACE IN SOLITUDE

Solitude—just the word can conjure up images of a lonely hermit or someone isolated on a mountaintop. But in reality, solitude is an essential aspect of a balanced life. It's not about being lonely; it's about finding peace and clarity within yourself. Embracing solitude can lead to profound self-discovery and personal growth.

In our hyper-connected world, it's easy to feel overwhelmed by constant interactions and the never-ending stream of information. Solitude provides a much-needed break from this noise, offering a sanctuary where you can reflect, recharge, and reconnect with your inner self. It's a time to step away from the demands of life and simply be.

Practical Advice

1. Schedule Regular Alone Time:
Treat solitude as a priority by scheduling regular alone time. This could be a few minutes each day or a dedicated block of time each week. Use this period to disconnect from the outside world—turn off your phone, step away from social media, and allow yourself to be fully present.

2. Use Solitude for Self-Reflection and Creativity:
Solitude is an excellent opportunity for self-reflection. Use this time to think about your goals, your values, and where you're headed in life. Journaling can be a helpful tool for organizing your thoughts and gaining insights. It's also a great time for creativity. Whether you're into writing, painting, or playing an instrument, solitude can spark creativity and allow your mind to explore new ideas without distractions.

3. Enjoy Activities That Bring Peace and Relaxation:
Engage in activities that help you relax and find peace. This could be anything from reading a good book, taking a long walk in nature, practicing yoga, or meditating. The key is to choose activities that

allow you to unwind and connect with your inner calm.

Benefits of Solitude

- **Self-Discovery:** Spending time alone helps you get to know yourself better. It's a chance to explore your thoughts, feelings, and desires without outside influences.

- **Improved Mental Health:** Regular periods of solitude can reduce stress and anxiety, promoting overall mental well-being. It provides a space to process emotions and find clarity.

- **Enhanced Creativity:** Without the constant buzz of external stimuli, your mind can wander and explore new ideas, leading to greater creativity and innovation.

- **Inner Peace:** Solitude allows you to cultivate a sense of inner peace and tranquility. It's a time to recharge and center yourself, making you more resilient to life's challenges.

Lesson #39

Finding peace in solitude leads to self-discovery and inner calm. By scheduling regular alone time, using

solitude for self-reflection and creativity, and
engaging in activities that bring peace and
relaxation, you can experience the profound benefits
of being alone. Solitude is not something to be
feared; it's a gift that provides the space for growth
and self-awareness. So, embrace the quiet moments
and discover the peace that comes from within.

LIVING AUTHENTICALLY

L iving authentically—sounds like one of those self-help buzzwords, right? But for a queer man in today's world, it's the key to surviving and thriving. It's about shedding the expectations of society and embracing who you truly are, flamboyant quirks and all.

Here's how embracing my true self has been a game-changer:

Growing up queer, I always felt like I was wearing a mask. There were endless layers of pretending, hiding, and fitting into boxes that weren't made for me. I remember desperately trying to blend in, from acting interested in sports (even though I'd rather be learning the choreography to janet jackson's new video) to dating girls because it was "normal." It was exhausting, and honestly, I was miserable.

The real turning point came when I moved out on my own. For the first time, I saw people living their truth without fear, and it was like a light bulb went off. Why was I still pretending? It was time to drop the act and start living authentically.

I began to embrace my identity fully. I started going to Pride events, connecting with the LGBTQ+ community, and expressing myself in ways I never dared to before—yes, that included wearing clothes that screamed "I'm here, I'm queer, get used to it!" It was liberating. Each step away from the closet was a step towards true happiness.

Practical Advice

1. Be True to Yourself and Your Values:
Reflect on what truly matters to you. Identify your core values and let them guide your decisions and actions. Living in alignment with your values brings a sense of peace and authenticity.

2. Let Go of Societal Expectations:
Society loves to tell us how to live, especially when it comes to conforming to heteronormative standards.

Politely tell those expectations to take a hike. Focus on what feels right for you. It's your life, and you have the right to live it on your own terms.

3. Embrace Your Unique Qualities:
Celebrate what makes you unique. Your quirks, your style, your identity—these are what make you, you. Embrace them fully and let your true self shine. The world doesn't need another cookie-cutter version of someone else; it needs the real you.

Benefits of Living Authentically

- **Genuine Happiness:** Living authentically brings a deep sense of satisfaction and joy. You're no longer living for others but for yourself.

- **Improved Relationships:** Authenticity attracts genuine connections. When you're true to yourself, you draw in people who appreciate and love you for who you are.

- **Personal Growth:** Embracing your true self allows you to grow and evolve in ways that are aligned with your inner truth. It's a continuous journey of self-discovery and empowerment.

Lesson #40

Living authentically leads to genuine happiness and fulfillment. My journey as a queer man taught me that being true to yourself and your values, letting go of societal expectations, and embracing your unique qualities can transform your life. Authenticity is the key to unlocking your full potential and living a life that feels truly yours.

So here's to living authentically, breaking free from the mold, and celebrating the wonderful, unique person you are. It's time to shine your light and live your truth, unapologetically and with great joy. After all, if Lady Gaga taught us anything, it's that you were born this way, and that's something to be proud of.

DAS IT

Alright, we've reached the end of this rollercoaster of a book, and what a ride it's been! If you've stuck with me this far, I owe you a drink. So let's take a moment to reflect on the journey we've shared, packed with lessons, laughs, and a fair share of WTF moments.

We kicked things off by embracing our imperfections. Let's face it, perfection is a myth, like a unicorn or a politician who keeps their promises. The real beauty lies in our quirks and flaws, those little things that make us, well, us. Remember, you don't have to have it all together—nobody does, and that's okay.

We tackled forgiveness next, and if you're anything like me, you've got a mental burn book full of grudges. But holding onto those only hurts us. Forgiveness is like finally cleaning out your fridge; it's not fun, but you feel so much lighter once it's done. And let's be real, nobody wants to carry around that much emotional mold.

Setting boundaries was a game-changer. Learning to say no is like discovering the cheat codes to life. It's empowering to reclaim your time and energy from people who treat you like a doormat. If someone can't respect your boundaries, hand them a map and let them find their way out of your life.

Then we found resilience, that inner badassery that keeps you going when life feels like a dumpster fire. Resilience is the superpower we all need, whether it's bouncing back from a breakup or surviving another family gathering where Aunt Karen grills you about your life choices.

Self-love? Oh, honey, that's a lifelong romance. It's about treating yourself with the kindness and respect you'd offer your best friend. You wouldn't tell them they're a failure for eating an entire pizza, so why do it to yourself? Own your awesomeness and celebrate every bit of progress, no matter how small.

Travel and exploration added spice to our lives. There's a big, beautiful world out there waiting to be discovered. Whether you're jetting off to exotic locales or playing tourist in your own city, stepping out of your comfort zone broadens your horizons and feeds your soul. And hey, even if you get lost, that's just another adventure.

Community and giving back highlighted the importance of solidarity. Whether it's rallying together after a disaster or just helping out a neighbor, being part of a community is like having an extended family who actually likes you. Giving back doesn't just help others; it enriches your life too.

Mindfulness and meditation taught us to find peace in the chaos. It's about taking a few moments to breathe and center yourself, especially when life feels like a never-ending episode of "Survivor." These practices help you stay grounded and calm, even when your mind is racing like it's on caffeine.

Health and wellness reminded us that taking care of our bodies and minds is non-negotiable. You can't pour from an empty cup, so make sure to fill yours first. Eat well, move your body, and don't forget to check in with yourself mentally. Self-care isn't selfish; it's essential.

Living authentically was the grand finale. As a queer man, I've learned that embracing who you are, without apology, is the key to true happiness. Ditch the masks and societal expectations. Be unapologetically you, with all your fabulous quirks and unique qualities. The world doesn't need more clones; it needs your authentic self.

As you close this book, remember that this journey doesn't end here. Life is an ongoing adventure, full of twists, turns, and unexpected detours. Embrace the lessons, keep growing, and never stop being curious. Be kind to yourself when you stumble, and celebrate your victories, no matter how small they may seem. Life isn't about reaching a final destination but savoring every moment along the way.

To everyone who has read these pages, thank you. You are enough, just as you are. Your journey, with all its highs and lows, is what makes you unique. Embrace it with courage and curiosity. In a world that often demands conformity, be brave enough to stand out, to be true to yourself, and to live authentically. Remember, the challenges you face are stepping stones to your growth. Each setback is a setup for a comeback. Each moment of doubt is an opportunity to reaffirm your worth.

As Dolly Parton, the queen of self-love and authenticity, once said, "Find out who you are and do it on purpose." Shine brightly, live boldly, and never stop

growing. Here's to your continued growth, happiness, and
the incredible adventure that lies ahead.

ABOUT THE AUTHOR

Meet S.Y. Vidal, an artist at heart who thrives on creativity. Whether drawing, painting, writing, or diving into the psychological thrills of a horror movie, Vidal lives for artistic expression. Oh, and let's not forget the cats—each one is a muse and practically part of the writing team.

While Vidal's degree might not be in psychology, it still hangs proudly next to his priceless artwork—both testaments to the school of life. Let's say his wisdom comes less from textbooks and more from a curriculum set by a harsh yet enlightening life journey. It's the advice you'd get from a friend who may not know Pi to the 20th decimal but knows how to piece together a broken soul. Vidal writes how he talks—no holds barred, heartfelt, and relatable. The aim? To dive deep but keep it real, just like a chat with an old friend who's seen it all.

When the pen is down, and the paints are packed away, Vidal immerses himself in the rich landscapes and vibrant culture of Puerto Rico. The island's natural beauty is not just a backdrop but a source of endless inspiration. Ultimately, Vidal stands by the mantra that the only person who can truly save you is yourself. It's a belief that anchors him and acts as the cornerstone of his work. Through his books, art, and voice, he empowers others to dig deep and discover their hidden wellsprings of strength.

YOUR VOICE MATTERS

If this book has been a companion on your healing journey, if it's helped you understand, process, or begin to heal from childhood trauma, I would be deeply grateful if you would take a moment to share your experience.

Your review isn't just words on a page—it's a beacon of hope for others who might be struggling, feeling alone, or searching for understanding. By sharing how this book touched your life, you could be the lifeline someone else needs to take their first step towards healing.

Would you consider leaving a review on:

- Amazon
- Goodreads
- Google Books

Every review, every shared story, has the power to make a difference. Thank you for being brave, for your journey, and for potentially helping another soul find their path to healing.

With gratitude & hope,

ALSO AVAILABLE